PAW PRINTS ON MY HEART

PAW PRINTS ON MY HEART

FROM BEING ABUSED FOR SIX YEARS TO FREEDOM

Giving a New Life to a Traumatised Rescued Puppy Farm Dog

MOLLY JEAN ROWE

YOUCAXTON PUBLICATIONS

OXFORD & SHREWSBURY

ISBN 978-1-911175-70-4
Printed and bound in Great Britain.
Published by YouCaxton Publications 2017

enquiries@youcaxton.co.uk

Dedicated to all dogs who have not found their special person yet
and to all the humans who have not yet found their special dog.
This book is for you.

Contents

When a dog buries its soul in your heart,
Treasure it, for you have been blessed.

Molly Jean Rowe

PROLOGUE

It is one of those very rare frosty November mornings, when the sky is deep blue and the air feels crisp and fresh. What a great day to be alive I am thinking to myself and as I watch my two dogs playing and rolling about in the frost, I feel sure that they are thinking the same. As I look on, I cast my mind back to twelve months earlier when the little Labrador dog that is now enjoying herself so much was just a thin nervous wreck who just wanted to curl up and hide. Oh, what a difference a year can make.

I would like to share with you my journey through the first twelve months of living with a rescue dog. It is a true story, telling of life as and when it happens, the ups and downs, the happy and sad times we share and how our bond with each other grows stronger and stronger.

PART ONE

A Plan Is Born

Twelve Months Earlier *September*

It is Friday – Friday the 13th to be exact – my husband and I are looking after our little grandson James. We have taken him to the pet shop to let him look at all the rabbits, hamsters, mice and fish that are there. He is in his element, so while he is engrossed, I wander over to the notice board, which is like a magnet to me; I love reading all the adverts about animals, dog-training lessons and all the various types of equipment that may be placed there. A couple of adverts catch my eye; they are dog rescue centres giving details of various dogs that need new homes. By this time John, my husband has also wandered over and I point them out to him.

"I think it's time," I say to him.

It has been about three years since we lost our German Shepherd dog Sasha. The grief was almost unbearable, but healing does come with time and I feel Sheba, our remaining German Shepherd, would really like to have a companion again; she was five years old when we lost Sasha. Sheba is a very nice, gentle soul that we re-homed when she was about eighteen months old. Of course, like all rescue dogs, she came with some problems, you expect that, after all no one lets go of the perfect animal, but with time and patience, she has become a dog to be proud of.

In the fifty years my husband and I have been married, our home has never been without a dog – and with four children, there was always a large variety of different animals for them to grow up with; dogs, cats, hamsters, rabbits etc. We believe that children should be around animals to experience the meaning of life, the love they share, the care in looking after them and of course the inevitable end of life of their little friend. It is a hard thing for them to learn but I would like to think it prepared them for the happy and sad times life may throw at them.

Most of the dogs in our life have been rescue dogs who were around eighteen months old when we re-homed them. I guess this is the age when dogs become troublesome as they are growing up and leaving their sweet little puppy stage behind. Often people cannot cope with the new, assertive, and possibly dominant dog they have in its place. Sadly, this is why the rescue centres are so full but lucky for people like us, who know that with time and patience these animals can turn out great.

My husband and I are getting on a bit now and realise our life will change quite a lot in the coming years; we are still very fit at the moment and I would like to think we have many more active years ahead of us, but it makes me wonder how many older dogs are out there? Dogs that no longer have the cute appeal of a younger dog; dogs that will struggle to find a forever home; that's what we will look for, a dog that due to its age or problems might make it very hard to re-home.

The Search Begins

After our grandson goes home, John types dog rescue centres into his computer and the first one to come up is The Dogs Trust in Evesham. As he flicks through the numerous photographs accompanied by details of each animal, he comes across a photo of a Labrador bitch. As he reads out the details to me, I feel they have been written with us in mind. She is a six-year-old breeding bitch that has been rescued from a puppy farm in Ireland. She is a very nervous traumatised dog who needs to go to a home with no children, preferably where someone will be at home with her all the time, and there must be another dog in the family, a nice laid-back animal who will help to give her confidence.

When I hear that she has been rescued from a puppy farm my heart goes out to her, I know she must have suffered terribly; she would have been living in awful conditions and just used as a puppy–making machine. When I think about the awful conditions poor battery hens used to live in, imagine how cruel it is to keep dogs that need to run, play, and enjoy human company, penned up in filthy cages, sometimes stacked on top of one another, never experiencing kindness, just abuse. As long as people buy a puppy without checking out the conditions they come from this sort of thing will carry on. If it was not for the RSPCA and centres like The Dogs Trust, these wretched creatures would never be re-homed, they would be cruelly disposed of when they were no longer able to do their job that is if they didn't die first. This little dog is one of the lucky ones, she's been rescued, and I know in my heart that if we end up with this dog, no one will ever hurt her again. John looks at me and says, "If we get a move on we can go and see her today".

I am not so sure. I know Evesham isn't that far away but we have to find the centre and time is against us. I don't need to give it too much thought though before I say, "alright let's give it a go" and we quickly get ourselves ready. We need to take Sheba with us so we put her into the car and set off. While we are driving, my mind keeps coming up with the date Friday the 13th – maybe it isn't such a good day to meet the little dog – maybe we should have left it until tomorrow but I also know deep down, that if we are going to help this dog then the sooner the better.

After taking the wrong turn several times, we at last arrive at The Dogs Trust Centre. John rushes into the reception while I unload Sheba. Are we in time? I'm not sure, but when John reappears he says we have about fifteen minutes until they close. They have taken his details and told him where we can find Winifred (that is the Labrador's name).

We have to walk down a very long driveway to reach the kennels. John stays with Sheba while I go and try to find the right pen to have a look at the dog. Of course, I have to pass several other dogs in their pens, most of who rush towards me, barking excitedly as I pass by. I come to the pen that I think is the one next to Winifred's, where there's a very excited Labrador with a bandage on its tail, barking nervously at me. I can feel my heart starting to beat faster; it's just a few more steps before hopefully I will meet our little girl.

However, all I see is a quick flash and an empty pen, as she disappears into her sleeping quarters. I call to her but there is no way she is going to show herself. I shout to John to come and have a look; "She's gorgeous," I laugh; "you're going to love her." He comes across but soon realises I am only joking. We both try to coax her into coming to see us but to no avail.

"We'll have to go and find someone to help us," he says. We tell the first Dogs Trust person we find about our problem and she says she will go and get Winfred and bring her out to us. She puts us in what I can only describe as an outside room with a fence all around, a bench to sit on and various things for the dogs to play with. It is a very safe place for people to meet their chosen dog for the first time.

Our First Meeting

We sit there for what seems an age, with Sheba wondering what all the fuss is about. Then the girl appears with a very reluctant dog dragging behind her. I will never forget the first image I have of the dog. She is not walking, she is crawling on all fours and she looks so small, so scared. We are both very shocked at what we are seeing, this animal has obviously suffered badly; she needs help and I hope we are the people that can give it to her.

We remain seated as she is brought into the pen. I'm nervous as to how Sheba will behave when they first meet; will she frighten her? Will she attack her? After all, a lot depends on Sheba; if they aren't compatible, we won't be able to adopt this dog. As Winifred is led in, Sheba is very curious and we keep her on the lead so she can introduce herself. I see Winifred's lips curl slightly and Sheba reads the signs and backs off. She knows this little dog is terrified and that she needs more time. Because of the dog's deep-seated fear of people, John sensibly stays in the background; we don't want to overcrowd her.

The girl sits with Winifred, who appears to be glued to her leg; she's not going to move an inch. I have time to take a better look at her now and I realise what a pretty little dog she is, looking much younger than her years. She's got a nasty scar by her right eye; much closer and I think she would have lost the eye altogether. Of course, it hadn't been treated, just left to heal on its own, which must have been extremely painful. There are several scars around her other eye but they're not so deep. While we are sitting there, the sun comes out from behind the clouds and the little dog lifts her head; her eyes squint as she looks towards the bright light and she seems to be enjoying the experience. I wonder if she has ever been able to feel the joy of the sun on her body in the horrible conditions she's been rescued from.

I would love to stroke her but I know it will only frighten her more. I have some tit-bits in my pocket and I try to tempt her but she is having none of it. The girl tells us she has had very little contact with people and what she did have would not have been a good experience for her. What an awful life this little dog must have had.

As we sit and chat to the girl, she tells us about another family that had shown an interest in Winifred but thought she would be too much for them to take on. She would need such a lot of time spent on her that they did not feel she was the right dog for them and as Winifred had taken an instant dislike to their dog, that had really made their minds up.

The girl also says that if we feel Winifred might be too much for us to cope with she could go and fetch the dog from the next pen to Winifred's for us to look at, the Labrador with the bandage on its tail. She also comes from the same puppy farm but is not such a nervous dog; she has had some of her tail taken off after gangrene had set in from an injury the poor animal had suffered.

Although I feel very sorry for her, I think she has a better chance of finding a home than Winifred as she appears much more outgoing; people would have a chance of coming and looking at her, not like poor Winifred who would probably bolt for cover whenever anyone passed her pen. Winifred could not sell herself like most of the other dogs at the centre; I think she would just cower in the background.

Dogs Who Found Their Way into Our Family

When I first met Sheba she well and truly sold herself to me. I didn't mean to get another dog at the time but went with my son Daniel, to our local re-homing centre to look at a large German shepherd that he was interested in. We met her in a well-fenced area where we were able to let her loose and play ball with her, just getting to know her. I was surprised that Daniel let me do all the playing while he just sat on a bench watching; I thought this was a bit strange, as he'd done nothing but talk about this dog for days. Well, she put on a good show, doing everything I asked her to do and I noticed that when other dogs walked past the pen, she showed an interest but that was all, there was no rushing about trying to get to them, she seemed quite happy to stay and play with me. I said to

Daniel what a super dog she was and I thought he should have her. He said he wanted Michelle his partner to come and look at her first and see if she liked her. Arrangements were made for me to return the next day with Michelle to see what she thought of her; I was sure she would love her; I knew I was falling for her.

The next meeting with Sheba was almost identical to the first, she didn't put a paw wrong and did everything I asked; she sat when I asked her to, she lay down and quite happily fetched the ball whenever I threw it for her, the show she put on was unbelievable. I felt sure Michelle would be impressed as she sat there watching from the same bench that Daniel had been sitting on the day before. However, when I went over to her she said Sheba looked rather scary and she was not sure she would feel comfortable with her.

That took me by surprise; I had not noticed that side of Sheba at all. All I could see was a very eager, fun loving dog who needed a home. I felt a lot of trust in her but I must admit deep down I was rather pleased that Michelle had not taken to Sheba because I knew then that she was coming home with me.

I wasn't sure what John would say; over the years he's come to know me well and never seems to be surprised when a new animal joins the family but at that time we already had three dogs, so taking on another one might have been expecting too much. However, I felt sure that when he met Sheba, he would get the same feeling I did and welcome her into our home. Our family of dogs at the time consisted of Bouncer, an elderly Labrador who came into our family when our son Mathew and his wife had their first baby and a very bouncy, boisterous dog was too much for them to cope with. He was a fun loving dog but also very mischievous and the training he had received had been very little, so we always found him to be quite a handful.

Then there was Fen the Border collie bitch, who did not have to sell herself to us, she just adopted us when she kept turning up in our garden. We found out she belonged to a local farmer and we took her back to him on numerous occasions. However, in the end, he must have got so fed up with her walkabouts that we heard he was going to take her to the local dog rescue centre to be re-homed. Of course, on hearing that we asked if we could have her and that's how she came to be part of our family.

I would like to think she came to us because she really wanted to live with us but realistically, I know the main attraction was Zorro, the very handsome German shepherd we had at the time. Their temperaments were identical; both wanted to be top dog but since Zorro was with us first, he was never going to give up his number one spot.

There were many fights in the beginning as they sorted themselves out but they turned out to be the best of friends when the pecking order was agreed upon. Zorro was the leader of the pack, Fen second in charge, with Bouncer bringing up the rear. As long as that order was maintained, there were no problems but if one of them tried to challenge the leadership, they were sharply reprimanded by Zorro and peace would reign again. Zorro and Fen were two very high-energy dogs, both needing plenty of activities to channel their energy, so agility and obedience lessons were high on the list. Of course, I was a lot younger in those days and was able to put in the time and energy they needed and it was well worth it, I had two fantastic dogs whose collection of rosettes and trophies I can still admire to this day.

Unfortunately, Zorro died at the age of nine from a brain tumour and it left a big empty hole in our lives, one I did not think we would ever be able to fill. However, it must have been about eighteen months later, when we were looking after our son's dog Bruno, also a German Shepherd, that I realised how much I missed having a Shepherd around. They have always been my favourite dog; I love their loyalty and the protective qualities they possess, so that is how a trip to the local dog centre came about.

Sasha was to fill the gap Zorro had left behind; yes, she sold herself to us but not in the normal way. She got our attention by charging at the pen and almost jumping the height of the compound, barking at us aggressively as we peered in at her. Someone has their work cut out with her I remember thinking but as I watched, I realised how much she reminded me of Zorro. She was also a small dog like Zorro but he never realised that he was small, confidence just oozed out of him. A police dog trainer once told me that Zorro would have made a good police dog. Size would not have mattered, he would have been able to do the business and I am sure he would; I always felt very safe when Zorro was around. Sasha on the other hand had a very nervous, almost hysterical bark. I felt she was at the end of her tether; she needed a home and quick. I knew we would be taking on a challenge but I felt she needed a chance so that's how Sasha became a new member of our family. It was nice to see Fen running around with her new friend and Bouncer did not have to feel he was the underdog any longer, as Sasha was never going to be the dominant dog that Zorro had been.

Life with Sasha was not easy as she had many problems; she was a very highly-strung dog and I wished we had known more of her history. We were told that she had a metal plate in her front leg, as it had not grown the way it should have but it was not until much later that we found out the truth, that she had been run over by a car. That explained a multitude of things; she was terrified of cars when they passed us on our walks, spinning round violently when she heard them approaching and once knocking me right off my legs. I never found the underlying course of the problem, it always puzzled me, but if I had known the truth things might have turned out differently.

Unfortunately, Sasha was not with us very long; she died prematurely before she reached the age of six, but in that time she did me proud by winning the Good Citizen gold award at the training classes I took her to. Only two dogs in the class qualified to win that award and she was one of them; I cannot tell you how proud I was of her. She had come to us with so many problems it would have been easy just to have written her off. The only regret I have is that we did not get more time together; I felt there was so much left for us to share but I would like to think John and I managed to give her a good and happy life in the short space of time we spent together. She was such a lovely dog who needed plenty of love and at least we were able to give her that.

There were no problems when Sheba joined the little pack of three, Bouncer, Fen and Sasha welcomed her, I think they sensed the lovely laid-back nature of the new addition and it was lovely watching all four dogs running around, enjoying each other's company. Unfortunately, it wasn't many months before Bouncer became ill and we lost him; it was a sad time but he was a very old dog and we knew it would happen at some point. We had hardly got over losing Bouncer, when we lost Fen, which was more of a shock; although she wasn't a young dog, we thought we would have her for a few more years.

We were then down to two dogs, Sasha and Sheba my two beautiful Shepherds but as I said earlier, Sasha died prematurely before she reached the age of six, so Sheba lost the last of her new found friends. It was a difficult time for us all, leaving John and I reeling from the shock of losing our little canine family and Sheba too, must have felt so alone now all her friends had left her. It took almost three years before we felt strong enough to look for another dog but we knew Sheba needed a companion and we would do our best to find the right one for her.

So as you can see when I first met Sheba she was able to sell herself to me and we connected. I don't think poor Winifred will ever be able to do that, she is too traumatised to show herself off. I cannot see this little dog finding a new home easily; I think she might be destined to spend the rest of her life in kennels.

There isn't much time to get to know Winifred in our first meeting but I find I can't take my eyes off her the whole of the time we are there; I'm transfixed. Whether she can feel me looking at her I don't know but for one very brief moment she turns her head and looks at me. Our eyes meet and this little dog doesn't need the power of speech, it's all in her eyes. In that split second I see fear, hopelessness and hurt but most of all, the message that will haunt me for the rest of my life; PLEASE HELP ME. I feel a shudder pass down my spine. Our souls meet and I know this connection will never be broken.

All too quickly, it is time to say goodbye but we arrange to come again on Sunday when we will have much more time with her. Sunday can't come quickly enough. I know this dog is for us

Sunday Arrives

The day arrives and I think this has been the longest two days I can remember. I can't stop thinking about the little dog, I just want to be with her and reassure her that she will never be hurt again. But what if it doesn't go well? Maybe they will think we are not suitable to adopt her; maybe Sheba, who was very good at the first meeting, will take a dislike to her this time or vice versa. John has to tell me to relax, we will only be able to do our best, and that is all we can do.

We put Sheba into the car and armed with a pack of cooked liver pieces to try to tempt Winifred, we set off. The journey seems to take forever. Sheba settles down in the back of the car; I think she knows we have driven too far to be taking her for a lovely long walk somewhere so she resigns herself to chilling out and leaves all the worrying down to us (clever dog).

When we arrive, we head straight to the reception area to tell the girl behind the desk that we have come to see Winifred as arranged. She is a nice girl with a friendly face and she phones down to the kennels to let someone know we have arrived.

Again, we walk down the long drive that leads to the kennels. Sheba is very alert and she can hear dogs barking. I know she can remember she has been before but things seem different today, there is more going on, more people about and more noise coming from the kennels.

When we reach the kennels, we go into another reception area to let them know we have arrived. We meet another girl and after giving Sheba a fuss, she takes us to the outside room again. Then she goes to collect Winifred. It is not very warm and I feel a bit shaky. I keep telling myself it is because I am feeling cold but I think it is nerves really. John and I are sitting on the bench with Sheba at our feet, when Winifred is led in, I hope she will remember she has seen us before but it is hard to tell; she is still glued to her handler's leg. After a little while we let Sheba loose, leaving her lead on just in case we have to dive in to stop a fight. She goes and sniffs Winifred, then walks off to explore her surroundings and there is a big sigh of relief all round.

I start to talk to the little dog. Then I produce a small piece of liver and offer it to her, she takes it from me and Sheba of course has one too. Then I offer Winifred another one and she takes it very cautiously from my fingers but that is all she can manage, I can't tempt her with anymore. It must be so difficult for her because of the very nervous state she is in but I feel as though we've had a little breakthrough and when she lets me stroke her, I am over the moon. The bond is forming.

When the session is over, we go back into the reception and tell the receptionist we would like to adopt Winifred. She tells us we have to attend a pre-adoption meeting where they will inform us what we can expect when adopting a rescue dog and offer us help and advice that will hopefully help the dog settle in as trouble-free as possible. The next pre-adoption meeting was to be held the coming Wednesday. My heart sinks; that is another three days I'm thinking but I know it's in the dog's best interest; after all, what some of these rescue dogs have been through, they need to get the best possible chance of finding the right home so we put our names down to attend the meeting. We will still be able to take Sheba and spend some time with Winifred before the session begins, so that makes the wait seem a little better.

The pre-adoption meetings are held in the evenings after the kennels have closed, so we allow enough time before the meeting to see the little dog again. We are taken to a small room that has been made out to look like a living room with settee and chairs inside. To get there we have to walk with Winifred and her handler. This is the first time we have been with her when she is being walked on a lead and she is scurrying all over the place. We can't walk by her side or behind her, as she is just too frightened; it is such an ordeal for her. Once inside the room, she settles slightly and the helper stays for a little while before leaving us alone. This is another first for us, as we haven't been left alone with her before and it feels good; Sheba is still behaving herself and has not shown any jealousy towards the dog. Winifred lets me talk to her and stroke her and I even manage to walk her around the room; I am happy with the progress we are making and John takes a photograph of me resting my hand on her; it is a photo I will always treasure.

When the girl comes back to take Winifred to the kennels, we put Sheba into the car and make our way to the area where the meeting is going to take place. There are two other families going to the meeting besides us and we all look in the same frame of mind, excited but a little worried at the same time.

The meeting lasts for about an hour; the speaker knows each of the dogs that are going to be adopted, so she is making suggestions that will hopefully help each new owner as the dogs all have different needs. We quickly become aware that our little dog is quite different from the rest. She has far more problems, things like not having any visitors in the house for at least a month, attaching a long lead to her collar so we can catch her if needed, not to let her loose in the garden because we might not be able to get her back. In addition, it might be a good idea to get her an indoor kennel, as her place of safety when needed, and of course, as she has never been house trained that could be quite a problem. The other owners are told it would be a good idea to take their dogs to training classes, but of course, we can't take Winifred, as she just wouldn't be able to cope. I have to agree with that, right now it's the last thing on my mind. It feels like we're about to adopt a young puppy, rather than a fully grown six year old and that's the way I will go about training her; go back to the beginning. After all, this dog has not had a normal life and she will have to learn all the things she should have been taught as a puppy. She doesn't even know what the inside of a house looks like and all the different sounds that come from a TV, phone and washing machine could all be too much for her to take in. Baby steps, I have to keep telling myself, just baby steps.

When it is time to leave, we are asked to come back for a one-to-one visit but not to bring Sheba with us this time. I guess they want to see how the dog reacts to us when Sheba is not around; we make an appointment for the next day. As we are driving home neither of us speak very much, I think we are just trying to digest all the things we have been told. Sheba lies in the back of the car quite relaxed, soaking up the atmosphere and I feel sure she is starting to look forward to getting a little friend.

The One-to-One

While I lie in bed, Winifred is on my mind (no surprise there) and I start to think about her name; I don't really like Winifred, so I am going to give her a new name. I suspect the kennels had named her as I doubt she had a name when they rescued her, so what will suit her? It is some time before the answer comes to me, SHY, of course! We can tell people she is just a little shy when they first meet her and maybe that will help them to understand her problem.

It will seem strange to be travelling without Sheba, I am sure she knows where we are going. She looks a little down when we close the door behind us, but I try to assure her we will not be too long, I hope she understands.

Once again, we arrive at The Dogs Trust and the weather is still being kind to us; another fine day. We take the opportunity to dispose of all our loose change into a wishing well at the entrance to the kennels before we go and tell them we have arrived for our one-to-one. Again, they phone for someone to come and collect us and we are taken to yet another very small room with a desk in one corner and another little area leading off where various things are being stored; we sit down and wait. Then in comes Shy who does not look so frightened this time; I think she is getting to know us. We are then left alone to try to really get to know one another. John has wisely stayed in the background on our past visits as we think that most of the ill treatment she has received has come from men. He thinks now it's time to come closer and talk to her but she just looks at him nervously and pushes up closer to my leg. I stroke her gently, telling her we are here to help her not harm her. She then turns and puts her little head on my arm. Oh, I could cry! This must have taken a lot of courage from her, and I feel very humbled. This is the moment I know without a doubt our bond will never be broken.

The Healing Touch

For many years, I have been very interested in Faith Healing and have often been to have healing to help treat various problems and found it to be a great help. So, when my animals have needed help, I have never hesitated in having a healer treat them. It always fascinates me watching them receive their treatment; the relaxed look that comes into their eyes and the relief they experience is amazing. People have often said to me it's all in the mind but I don't agree, animals can't imagine the relief they are getting, they just get it, and they are always up for more. That makes it good enough for me; I know healing works.

However, it wasn't until four years ago when I had to have a major operation to deal with a deep seated brain aneurysm, that I found that I also had the gift. I did a lot of relaxation and meditation after my operation to try to help my body recover from its ordeal. It must have helped as I made a full recovery and it wasn't many weeks before I was up and enjoying life again. I was able to go and visit my horses and walk Sheba in the lovely fresh air; life was very precious to me now and I was out to enjoy it. On one of our walks, I noticed Sheba was limping slightly. I stroked her shoulder and was surprised to feel pain run through my hand. I kept it on her and felt my hand get very warm and tingly. Sheba seemed to enjoy what I was doing so I kept my hand there – could I be experiencing the feeling healers get, I asked myself? I hoped so; I would love to be able to give help to my family and animals. I felt a deep feeling of calmness come over me; a wonderful feeling. I was sure something was passing from me to Sheba, who lay down on her side, gave a deep sigh, and lay there until I felt it was time to finish; we then carried on and finished our walk. I felt tired but very happy and Sheba seemed more relaxed and looser than she had in the first half of our walk. The next day there was no sign of a limp and I knew then that I had been able to help her; this was the beginning of my healing journey.

So, while I am sitting stroking Shy, I start to let my hand slowly run over her rigid little body, feeling for any pain she may have. I can feel she has pain in her head, ears and across the shoulders, so I start to give her healing, it is the only thing I can do that hopefully will give her some relief.

We are enjoying our time with Shy and are in no hurry to leave. Various helpers pop in from time to time to see how we are getting on and then a woman comes in and sits down at the desk. She has a folder with all Shy's information in it. She tells us of all the treatment Shy has been given since being with them. She has of course been neutered; she had to have her teeth scraped to remove the plaque that had built up on them; and she has an ear infection that she is still having treatment for. In addition, she has been treated for a nasty skin infection.

We then talk about when we will be able to take her home. This had been discussed on one of our earlier visits and it had been decided that they would bring her to us as she is such an extreme case, but today we ask the question – will we be able to take her home ourselves? The woman says she will go and check for us, and on returning tells us we can take her home on Sunday if we want. You bet we want – we want nothing more.

She leaves us alone again to finish our time with Shy; I decide to walk her around the room and it feels good, I think she is starting to want to be with me.

"John open the door and we'll take her onto the grass outside." As soon as he opens the door, Shy dashes out like a wild animal, taking me by surprise but luckily, I'm able to keep hold of the lead, for this little dog is very strong. I know I can't loose her, as we will never catch her again. Instinct tells me to drop to the ground and as soon as I do Shy nervously comes to me. Phew what a relief! Just a little taste of things to come, I think to myself. Hurry up Sunday, she needs a proper home where she can learn to trust and relax in safety.

There are mixed feelings on the way home; we are very excited to know we will be bringing our little girl home on

Sunday but we also know it will not be a picnic in the park, there is such a lot for us to learn. We want to give her the very best we can but are we going to be capable? We have already had a taste of things to come when she turned from being the most timid dog in the world to a wild thing as she dragged me out of the door. We will have our work cut out for us that is for sure, but deep inside I know we are capable. We can at least give her plenty of love, something she has never had.

Saturday is mainly spent getting everything ready for the new arrival. I manage to borrow an indoor kennel from a friend and we decide to set it up in the rear porch leading from the kitchen. The weather is still very good for the time of year, so we know she will not get cold. Although she won't be in the house with us, she will be able to relax in the safety of her kennel and will still be able to hear all the different noises and voices coming out of the kitchen. We line the kennel with plenty of newspaper and then put blankets in to keep her nice and cosy. We clear out the rest of the porch so she can get out of her kennel and have a little wander around if she wants, and of course go to the toilet. As she has never been house trained, I imagine this could take a long time, so we have to prepare ourselves for that.

When we are both satisfied that we have done all we can in the porch, our thoughts turn to the journey home. We decide that I will travel in the back of the car with her. It is fortunate that two of our back seats fold down just leaving one seat in position which means that we can fit a dog basket where the seats would have been, enabling me to sit and hold her as we travel; that is of course if she will stay in the basket. Sheba seems very interested in what we are doing, I think she realises Shy is coming home and she too is picking up on our excitement.

"Not long now girl" I say as I stroke her, "soon you will have a little friend".

Everything is in place now – all we need is the day to arrive. It feels a lot longer than ten days since we first met the little dog, the frightened cowering little creature who has melted our hearts. Soon she will be in our life, a family to fold their arms around her and protect her for the rest of her life, be it long or short; she will have the best we are able to give her.

Sleep doesn't come easily for me tonight and morning seems to be a long time coming, but when it gets here, I'm happy to see it is another fine day. The sun is shining and it seems one of those happy days that come along every now and again; nothing to do with the mood I am in of course, it is just a good day.

PART TWO

The Homecoming

Our Adventure Begins

The journey to The Dogs Trust is filled with mixed emotions – excitement, apprehension – we just do not have a clue what we are letting ourselves in for. However, Shy isn't the first rescue dog we have owned and I am sure she won't be the last; we will just draw on our experiences and do the best we can.

When we arrive, we check in at the main reception and are given a form to sign to say we want to re-home the dog and then we pay the adoption fee. A folder is handed to us with all Shy's information inside and an envelope marked Vets Records, detailing all the treatment she has received whilst in their care. There is a vaccination card with information of all the injections she has had, and when they will be due again. She has been micro-chipped and we are given the document with her special number... On top of this, she will get four weeks free veterinary insurance. Because she is underweight, we are advised to give her small feeds several times a day and we are given a bag of the food she has been fed so as not to upset her stomach with a sudden changeover.

All Dogs Trust dogs leave with a collar and lead but we want to buy her a harness to wear as well; knowing how strong she was when she pulled me out of the door, we do not want her to damage her neck if she did it again. We tell the receptionist that we want to buy a harness for Winifred and she says she will send a message to the kennels so they can find the correct size harness for the dog to wear; we are given a bag to put everything in including various leaflets we have chosen which we think might come in handy.

The woman then picks up the phone and phones down to the kennels reception. She says, "Winifred's family have arrived and they will be coming for her shortly". What a buzz: "Winifred's family"–it sounds lovely! Of course, we know her as Shy now but that does not matter.

This time we are allowed to drive down to the kennels, as we will be picking the dog up. Before we leave the car, we spray the inside with a de-stressing and calming spray, which is supposed to help your pet at times like this. We both take in some deep breaths in case it works for us also; however, the smell is not very pleasant. However, I hope the dog will get something out of it.

When we enter the reception we are surprised to see Shy is already there, standing by a girl at the desk and looking very smart in her new harness. We sit down quite close to her hoping she will come to us but no chance. It is then explained to us what treatment she needs for her ears and we're given a lotion that needs to be put in her ears every other day until it clears – that'll be fun, I'm thinking! Then in two weeks' time, we have to take her to the vet to have her ears checked. All is sorted and it's time to say goodbye and put Shy in the car. I ask if one of the young helpers can lift her into the car for us, as I know she will not get in by herself. I sit in my seat first and Shy is then carefully lifted in. The lead is given to me and Shy cautiously crawls into the basket. John starts the engine and drives slowly and carefully out of the dog centre; Shy is on her way home.

The journey goes better than we expect. Shy lies very still in her basket and as I stroke her, I give her some healing; she doesn't seem to mind and the more I give her, the more she relaxes – I think she is quite enjoying it. John keeps asking, "Is she alright?" I think he is quite amazed at how quiet she is.

The journey goes really well but it's quite a relief when we arrive home and Shy's new life can now begin. I attach Sheba's long training lead to Shy's collar; the plan is that John will open the rear car door while I hold Shy; I will then pass him the lead while I get out of the passenger door. I will walk to the back of the car and take hold of the lead, so we can get her out safely. Well the first half of the plan goes well; John has the lead and I open my door to get out – What we do not expect is that when Shy spots the open passenger door, she makes a bolt for it and because she is on the end of a long lead John can't stop her. Luckily, I am able to catch hold of the lead; I know if she gets free, she could end up on the road as there are no gates to stop her. We have to get her into the garden and then if she does get loose, there is less chance of her hurting herself as we have made the garden very secure.

After a bit of a commotion we make it into the garden, more by luck than anything else and now things are more on my side but because she is on a very long lead, she is able to run round and round me. If you have ever lunged a very young, excited horse, you will know what I'm dealing with; for a little dog, her strength is hard to believe. At least when you lunge your young horse you've had months and sometimes years to get to know your animal; they get to know your voice and they start listening to you after the first rush of excitement has passed. But – Shy is not a horse and she hasn't had any time getting to know and trust us. All she wants to do is run away in blind fear. John stands by watching helplessly, there is nothing he can do. I am starting to get a little giddy, and then I think will it work if I drop to the ground as I had done at the centre? Anything is worth a try because I am starting to worry about the lead breaking or me losing my grip. I go down on my knees, quietly calling to Shy as I do and her reaction is almost instant; she stops and once more crawls on her belly to come to me. What a relief – my heart is pounding and I am shaking but we have overcome our first obstacle, the first of many I guess.

After a few moments, I slowly rise to my feet, talking quietly to her as I do. This time I have the lead short so I have more control if she decides to do the whole lunging thing again, and sure enough she tries to make another bolt for it but she cannot get very far this time. I feel so sorry for this little girl, what on earth has she had done to her to make her so terrified? We need to get this dog's trust and the sooner the better for her own sake.

I slowly move towards the bench, thinking she might feel a little happier if we are sitting down; it seems to work and she starts to settle a little. I look at John and wonder if he is thinking the same as me. Have we taken on too much? Are we capable of turning this little girl's life around? All I know is we will try our very best, she deserves that, after all her life up to now has been having puppies, making money for undeserving people who should have been looking after her, not abusing her. She should have bonded with humans, not be terrified of them. She has given her all and got nothing back but misery. I can't help thinking of all the other poor creatures that are still living the same life that she has had. The banning of puppy farms cannot come quickly enough for me.

As we sit on the bench, we talk quietly to her, trying to reassure her that we will not hurt her and after a while, she starts to take a little interest in her surroundings, looking slowly around, her little nose starting to sniff in the air. The weather is being very kind to us, so it is very pleasant just sitting here; John and I both need the time to relax a little and take in the moment.

Meeting Her Big Sister

The next big step in Shy's life is to introduce her again to Sheba. We are not sure how it will go, after all this is Sheba's territory; will she take to Shy being on her home ground? She has been so good with her up to now but are things about to change? So much depends on Sheba – we need her to be good.

John goes into the house and brings Sheba out on her lead just in case there is a problem. She spots Shy and she looks alert, ears pricked, pulling slightly on the lead. John walks her to us; she sniffs Shy all over and then leaves her alone. She will make a good sister for the little dog; she will be able to show Shy how to relax and have fun. Sheba will be able to teach her things we will not be able to – in fact, she will show her how to be a dog.

John lets Sheba off her lead and she walks and sniffs around the garden, coming over now and again to check Shy out. Shy watches her carefully and I wonder what must be going through her mind. I give her a little walk around the garden; she is so jumpy, everything frightens her and I have to move very slowly so as not to scare her but she is walking with me – something she would not have done earlier in the day – so we are making progress. John and I are happy with that.

The rest of the day is spent mostly in the garden. We attach a long lead to Shy and let her wander around, lead dragging behind her just in case we need to catch her quickly. I don't think she is happy with the lead trailing behind her because it makes her quite jumpy but given the advice we had from Dogs Trust, we think we should follow their instructions; after all, we need everything to be on our side. I think the highlight of the day is when she goes and has a wee; it is funny what things get you excited isn't it? Sheba looks at us strangely; she doesn't understand why we are making such a fuss.

When evening starts to fall, we think it's time to introduce her to her sleeping quarters. On seeing the kennel, she jumps straight in and goes as far back as she can get, curling up very tightly in one of the corners as if she is trying to make herself invisible. I leave the kennel door open, so she can get out for a drink and eat the food we've left for her and of course go to the toilet if she needs to. As she has never been house trained, we hope she will use the newspapers we have put down and not the inside of her kennel. We say our goodnights and leave her alone. I think after the busy day she has had, she will appreciate the chance to quietly lie and digest the day's events.

When we go to bed, we wonder what sort of night we are in for – will she be frightened in her new surroundings, will she howl or bark? As we live in a bungalow, our bedroom is only across the hall from the back porch where she is sleeping, so we will be able to hear any sound she might make; we prepare ourselves for a restless night.

A New Week a New Life

I wake in the early hours, surprised that we have had a good night's sleep, with no noise from Shy. I lie there thinking about what the day might have in store for us; the sun is starting to break through, so it looks as if we are in for another nice day, Great! We will be able to spend a lot of time outside again. It's a good place to get to know Shy and she seems a little more relaxed when she is not confined; I think she doesn't feel so trapped.

I get up earlier than usual; I couldn't wait to meet the little dog again. I take Sheba out through the front door and walk her round to the back garden. I don't want her to walk through the back porch until I have had a chance to see to Shy.

I then go into the porch, talking quietly to let Shy know it's me, I can see she has eaten her food and has gone to the toilet on the newspaper; so far so good, this is a good start to the day. I peer into the cage and can see she is still curled up as far back as she can get, her little eyes look into mine and what I see is a mixture of fear and recognition; she looks as if she wants to greet me but does not have the confidence. I chat quietly to her as I clean up. "Don't worry little girl, you have done nothing wrong." I try to keep it very upbeat, I want her to know I am happy, not cross with her and to let her know how much I love her.

After I finish cleaning up, I fetch Sheba back into the house and start to make her breakfast; I am going to feed Shy before I try to take her outside. Sheba has her breakfast in the kitchen and I put Shy's in the porch and then leave her to eat it, knowing she will not eat if I stay with her. I stand and watch from the kitchen window and after a few minutes, she ventures out of her kennel and eats her breakfast. I have never seen an animal eat so quickly before, she just bolts the food down as if she is expecting someone or something to jump out at her. I wonder if she thinks it is a trap, had she been caught like that before. If this dog could talk, I think we would be amazed at what sort of things had happened to her, will she ever be able to trust anyone?

After half an hour, I return to the porch, sit down on the step, and start talking to her again. I notice that she has taken her lead, which I had left hanging in the porch, into the kennel and I wonder why she has done that. Is it because it has her scent on it, or maybe she is lonely? After all, she would have had puppies with her most of her life; I must sort her out some toys for tonight.

I carry on talking to her softly, hoping she will come out of her kennel, so I can attach her lead and we can have a little walk outside but she doesn't trust me enough yet; I will have to reach inside the kennel and get hold of her collar to gently pull her out. It crosses my mind that she might snap at me but there is nothing else I can do, she is not going to come out any other way. As I pull on the collar, she very reluctantly edges forward.

"Good girl Shy, you're doing great," I said, giving her lots of praise.

Finally, she is out of the kennel but she's very nervous and her tail is tightly tucked under her so that it almost looks as if she hasn't got one. However, she has not shown any sign of aggression, which can only be good.

With the lead attached, I open the porch door, fully expecting to be pulled forward at great speed but Shy holds back this time – she's not sure of her surroundings so she lets me go first and I have to gently pull on the lead to get her to follow me. We are in the back garden now and I know I must make sure she doesn't get away from me; it isn't as secure as the front garden and there are several places where she can escape if she breaks free.

Seeing Shy walked at the dog centre, I remember they had her on a long lead and she was able to move whichever way she wanted, so I am going to do the same. I give her the length of the lead and let her rush in front, behind, or off to the side. I let her do whatever she wants; after all, she has never been trained to walk on a lead. She is like a puppy, learning things for the first time in her life but a puppy would not have all the hang-ups this poor dog has. I feel it is right to train her in the same way I would train a very young animal, plenty of praise, plenty of tit-bits and hopefully, with time, she will learn to trust me and with trust, I believe the rest will follow.

After our walk, I put Shy back into the porch, close the door and take off the lead; she immediately shoots back into her kennel, her place of safety. I feel pleased with how things went; she can relax now and I can go and have a nice cup of tea.

About mid-morning, after Shy has had her second small meal, I think maybe now is the time to have a go at cleaning her ears. I'm not looking forward to it as I am not sure she trusts me enough yet but I need not have worried, she is very good and lets me do all that I have to do; I think she knows it is to make her better. Afterwards I take her into the front garden along with Sheba and let her loose; John and I sit and watch the two dogs getting to know one another. It is lovely to see Shy exploring her surroundings, sniffing the grass, acting more like a dog, even going to the toilet. She seems to be getting to know her name, or is it the sound of my voice? We even get a little wag of the tail; things are progressing nicely.

In the afternoon, we think the time is right to introduce Shy to the inside of the house. Fully aware of all the strange objects and noises she is about to experience, we make sure not to have the TV too loud, or use the washing machine; we will try to keep things as quiet as possible until she gets more comfortable with the situation.

Leaving her on the long lead, we let her loose; Sheba is there to give her confidence, so all we have to do is sit and watch. The lead is hindering more than helping her – she keeps getting it caught around various objects such as table and chair legs. Every time it happens it frightens her, so I tell John I'm going to take it off' and he agrees; after all there is nowhere for her to run, as she can't get out of the room. She seems a lot more settled without it dragging behind her and she carries on exploring every nook and cranny. While she is in the house I take the opportunity to give her some more healing; she is a little tense but she doesn't object.

I think we can say our first real day with Shy has gone very well, much better than we dared hope for. I do however hold my breath when Shy puts her nose into Sheba's dish while Sheba is eating, I thought a fight might break out but no, Sheba just let her carry on with not even a growl; we have a dog in a million, she is a star.

Tonight when I put Shy to bed, I give her a couple of Sheba's old cuddly toys, just in case I am right about her missing her puppies; however in the morning, I find she has bitten their heads off, so I guess she's not missing her puppies that much after all!

Time for Sheba

Because Sheba has been behaving herself so well, we think she deserves a treat so we are going to take her to The Worcester Countryside Centre; she loves going there where she's free to explore and meet other people with their dogs. We always enjoy ourselves too; it's a very relaxing place to be and when you leave the children's play area behind, there are just large well fenced fields for your dog to explore. So after seeing to all Shy's needs we leave her to enjoy a little peace and quiet, and she looks quite relaxed curled up in her kennel.

We all have a good time at the park; John and I are able to relax, something that we have not been able to do much of lately. We watch our beautiful dog happily tracking scents, running backwards and forwards, chilling out in her own little world.

"I wonder if we will ever be able to bring Shy here John?" I say, "It would be lovely to watch the two dogs running around together". I can see from his expression that he doesn't think it will happen for a long time yet, if ever.

Driving home, I start to worry a little about Shy being left on her own; although we have not been away very long, it's the first time she has been left and I hope she has not been too stressed, as I really can't bear to think of her being upset. When I peer into her kennel, I am relieved to see her little face looking back at me; she almost manages a wag of her tail and she doesn't look as if she has been worried. I am very relieved.

The rest of the day is spent seeing to Shy. She has started to come out of her kennel more, making things easier as I don't have to pull her out so much. I decide that any training I give her will be off the lead. I know it is against the advice we have been given from Dogs Trust, but this little dog has been a prisoner, either being tied up or kept in a cage and I feel to earn her trust, she needs to be free to make her own decisions. If something does frighten her she will be able to run away, not yank her neck as she pulls to escape I know I will be taking a chance but something tells me it is the right thing to do.

The Training Begins

We take the dogs onto the front lawn, Shy and Sheba both free. Armed with a little bag of goodies I start to call Shy to come to me and of course, Sheba comes, followed closely by Shy; clever Sheba is showing her what to do. I start to walk around the garden calling Shy to me; the little dog comes several times and walks a few strides by my side – it feels great!

"She is learning," I say to John and he nods; I think he is impressed.

After we finish our bit of training, I make a lot of fuss of Shy and then retire to the bench to just sit and watch the two dogs. Sheba tries a couple of times to have a little play, I think Shy would like to play but she is too nervous at the moment. Her toilet training is still going well and she is learning to go outside more.

A chill starts to come into the air so we take the dogs into the house and this time we leave all the doors open to see if Shy would like to explore the other rooms and explore she does, not missing out any room. This must be like a completely new world for her. It's lovely to see her walking around, even though any different or sudden noise sends her into fright mode. Everything we do has to be done in slow motion – we have to walk slowly when she is close by, and she is terrified of anything above her, so if I am carrying a plate; or if either one of us coughs she dashes off and I think she is on the brink of a nervous breakdown. She needs time and very careful handling to help bring her out of it; she's had six long years to get into this state, so there will be no quick fix but time is something we have plenty of.

Drawing on Past Experiences

As I mentioned before we keep horses; five in fact, three horses and two ponies. One of the ponies reminds me a lot of Shy for he too had a bad experience early on in his life. He was bought when he was young, to hopefully be a riding show pony for our friend's capable young daughter. As he had not been backed to be ridden when they bought him, they sent him away to be broken in. He was a very nice natured little animal so they didn't expect there would be any problems. You can imagine how shocked they were when told he was unbreakable and would be of no use to them. The animal they got back was very different to the pony they had sent away; he was very nervous and jumpy when around people, not allowing anyone to catch him when he was loose in the field. Although they tried to get his confidence back again, it was of no use, he would no longer be the perfect partner for their daughter, so they came to the decision to sell him.

Hearing about the pony's predicament and being quite a soft touch, I went to see him. He was a very handsome little chap with fantastic movement and a kind but scared look in his eyes and I felt for the little fellow. I had no need of a 13.2 hh pony but I think he needed me. I don't think he would have been able to cope with a young handler; he needed someone with patience and the time to let him recover from his ordeal, so I decided to buy him.

I felt he was on the brink of a nervous breakdown much like Shy, so when we put him in the field we let him loose; "go and chill out little fellow", I said. We did not expect or want him to be doing anything for a while anyway; I just had a good feeling that when we needed to catch him, he would let us.

As luck had it, Lady, the pony we already had (a little old rescue), took to the little chap instantly and he followed her everywhere. She was his rock; it was what he needed, just like Shy with Sheba. The pony's name was Harry but we renamed him Frisbee as it suited his personality. In the weeks that followed, on a good day Frisbee allowed us to get close to him although he was still very tense if his back or head were touched. I feel sometimes nice natured animals don't always get the best deal; because they seem to learn quickly, some people push them on before they are mentally ready and then get cross with them when the animal starts to play up. They think they are being naughty, out of character and just trying it on; they blame the animal and don't stop to look at the whole picture; maybe if they took a step backwards sometimes, they might go forward a lot faster.

I believe this is what had happened to Frisbee; you would be hard pushed to find a kinder, gentler little pony and it would never enter his head to bite or kick you. I believe he had been pushed too hard, not given time to get his head around the things he was being taught. The people who said he was unbreakable were really covering up for their own incompetence. The great pity is they spoilt the life of a truly lovely pony, as even now he has the odd flashbacks and goes to run away when we approach. Times like that are getting fewer though and we have never been unable to catch him (he also has allowed us to ride him).

When I look back to the early days of owning Frisbee, I realise how far he has come and I am truly convinced given time, patience and understanding, Shy will also come good. I doubt if she will ever really trust people and will never be able to let go of the cruelty she has received but one thing is certain; she has bonded with me and I with her and that alone will hopefully make a better life for her.

Moving in

Tonight I am woken up by Shy barking; I haven't heard her bark before and it seems so weak, as if she is frightened to be heard, maybe she had been shouted at in the past. She doesn't bark for very long and Sheba doesn't join in, so I think it is best to leave her alone and the rest of the night passes peacefully.

I am starting to take Shy out more in the back garden now. It's actually more like a field than a garden, and we have stables and a paddock for the horses to use which are very useful if one of them might need to be stabled for whatever reason, like seeing the vet or dentist, or just coming home for a holiday as I call it. They do seem to love coming, as they know they get a lot of T.L.C.

I have much more trust in Shy now, she follows me everywhere, and I don't worry that she might try to run off. She is also starting to play more with Sheba and it's so good to watch; a few days ago she would have been frozen to the spot, while now she is trying to be more like a dog and enjoying it.

The Dogs Trust phoned up today to see how we are getting on with the dog. Are we having any problems? Do we need any help or advice from them? I honestly could not think of anything; so far, life with Shy is turning out to be much better than I had expected and it feels good to say how happy we are with her. I should imagine they are surprised, I feel they half expected to get Shy back but that thought never crossed my mind. When we went to collect her, I vowed she would never go back; I know she was very well looked after while she was in their care, but nothing can replace a real family life, where she will receive individual love and attention and the chance to live life to the full.

I thank the lady very much for phoning and think how good it is that they have taken the time to follow up on the dog's progress. She also gives me a phone number I can ring if I need any help, which I find very reassuring.

We decide to put Shy's kennel in the house tonight; we are lucky that we have a small utility room next to the kitchen, into which the kennel will just about fit, so that although she will be in the house, she will still have her place of safety to hide in if she needs to. Sheba sleeps in the kitchen so she will not be too far from her. We dismantle the kennel and set it up inside the house; it's a tight squeeze but we manage it. The rest of the day is spent taking Shy out regularly to try to get her toilet trained and to let her run free, so hopefully, she will start to realise she is no longer a prisoner.

Meeting Buffy

Caroline, our daughter grows plants and has a small area at the back of our house to run her business, she comes every day and brings her re-homed greyhound Buffy with her. She is a lovely dog but today, meeting Shy for the first time, you can only say its instant dislike on her part. Buffy never stops barking at Shy and it is not a friendly bark. Shy is terrified, and quickly bolts and hides in the back porch. What a shame, things have been going so well. It makes me realise that we have been very lucky with Sheba, not all dogs are like her. Nevertheless, I'm sure that with time, Buffy will come to accept Shy and you never know, they may even become the best of friends one day.

When night-time comes, we introduce Shy to her kennel and she quickly jumps in.; there is never any problem in getting her to go into the kennel, it is her place of safety after all. We put a bowl of water inside the kennel this time as we are going to shut the door, just in case there is any trouble between the dogs in the night. We say our goodnights and leave the dogs in peace.

Again, I am woken in the night by Shy's barking but this time it is much louder and goes on for a lot longer. I decide to get up to see what is wrong with her, and try to think, what is different, why has she taken to barking. The only thing I can come up with is that we have shut her door, so after checking that everything else seems to be all right with her I open the kennel door and go back to bed; I do not hear another sound.

This morning when I go into the kitchen, I spot that Shy has done a wee. This might have been what all the barking had been about in the night, she had wanted to get out of her kennel and she couldn't. Maybe it is time to put her into a dog basket instead of the kennel, so she will be free to come and go whenever she wants. The dogs got on well together through the night so I don't think there is anything to worry about there. Later that day we fold up the kennel ready to be returned to the friend that we had borrowed it from. I sort out a basket (there are plenty to choose from, with all the dogs we have owned in the past) and put the blanket she has been lying on into the basket, as it will have her scent on it. Instead of putting the basket into the small room off the kitchen, we put it into the porch where her indoor kennel had been; I feel this is the best place to first introduce her to the basket. I call Shy to me as I sit on the step; she looks very unsure: her place of safety has gone and I'm not sure she trusts me enough yet to get into her basket. I keep talking to her trying to reassure her, and then I tap the basket saying "Come on Shy". To my amazement, she jumps into the basket, gosh that turned out easier than I expected.

Later in the day, while I am taking Shy on one of her little outings, John puts the basket into her sleeping area off the kitchen. I have introduced her to it several times during the day and she is now getting quite used to it so we think she will appreciate having her place of safety inside the house where she can go, when she feels the need.

Since being with us, she has spent a good deal of her time in the kennel. I guess that's the life she's always known, it would have been her place to live, eat, sleep and bring her puppies up in no wonder she finds it difficult to break the mould. The outside world would seem very scary to her and she must feel like a prisoner being set free after years in jail. But what had Shy done to be put in jail? She had not broken any laws; she had not stolen or harmed anyone; she was just a cute little dog, whose sole purpose was to make money for unfeeling people. She was not given the respect and caring she so desperately craved.

I feel that giving her a basket instead of an indoor kennel will be the first steps to get Shy to accept the outside world and be free to come and go without any hidden motives; I hope her life is about to change for the better.

Apart from taking her out for toilet training (which is coming on well), Shy is spending a good part of the day in the house with us now. She is still extremely nervous, every slight sound or sudden movements make her bolt for her basket but at least she is going there, so she has accepted it as her place of safety. When we sit down to watch the T.V in the evening (we still keep the volume down low) Shy is starting to come to me of her own free will and is starting to lick my hands, in her little way, I think she is trying to say thank you to me. I am possibly the only person she has ever been able to show any affection to, and I feel very honoured.

Before putting the dogs to bed, I always take them into the garden for their last outing of the day and as I open the kitchen door tonight, both dogs run out of the door together, something I had not expected to see for some time yet, it's a happy moment.

Time to Lead

It's Friday and there is a bit of a setback; Shy doesn't want to come into the house and no amount of coaxing seems to work. I can't help thinking that things have been going too well – it had to happen. I don't want to force her to come in so I think maybe if I get her more used to walking on a lead, she might learn to trust me enough to follow me if a situation like this occurs again. She has proved she is starting to trust me when she is free, as she walks quite nicely by my side, but at some point, she will need to have a lead on, so I feel it is now time to start her training.

I start by putting her lead on and off to get her used to me clipping it to her collar. You might think that this would be easy but more than likely, the only time she has worn a lead was when she was being forced to do something she was frightened of. I want to show her that nothing bad is going to happen, that she is not expected to do anything. At first she is very tense and just freezes; I stroke her gently and talk quietly to her as I clip and unclip the lead and after a while, she starts to relax. I think now is the right time to encourage her to follow me into the garden. She lunges forward a few times but I keep her lead short, not long, as I had done in the early days. I am talking to her in the same way as I do when she is free, telling her what a good girl she is when she walks by my side. She starts to settle and is walking more and more at heel. I keep the lesson short as I am very happy with how things are coming on and when the lesson is over, I let her loose to have a little run around with Sheba. As I watch, it amazes me to see how much she resembles a puppy, it is as if she is shedding the years and going back in time, living the early years she had so sadly missed.

It turns out that Friday is a good day after all, Shy is starting to come into the house again and I end the day by giving her more healing and then leave her content and curled up in her basket. I am sure she will have a good night's sleep, I know I will.

Saturday morning starts well; I am delighted to see that my kitchen has not been used as a toilet, so I quickly take the dogs outside and am very encouraged to see Shy perform; Great! She is getting the idea, she has been with us for less than a week and for a dog that has never been house trained, she is doing remarkably well. I know we will have many more accidents, but she is a bright little girl so I am beginning think it won't take too long.

When it's time to come back into the house, she is reluctant again, she does eventually come in, but it takes a lot of coaxing. So I put her basket back into the porch to see if that will help the situation, and sure enough, she jumps straight in, so I think I will leave it in there during the day. I don't want to distress her and if she is happier to be out there at the moment, that's fine by me. We have lots of small sessions of heelwork during the day and she is coming on great but is still very jumpy around my feet, I think she thinks I am going to kick her.

Animals may not be able to talk to us but if we really observe their behaviour, we will get to understand what they are trying to tell us; Shy has been kicked, that is obvious. She's had things thrown at her (she cowers when we carry anything in our hands.) and she's been hit with a stick (she runs off if you hold anything that resembles a stick.) She's been shouted at (she cowers if we raise our voices) and if either one of us coughs, she shoots off and hides. These are just a few of her hang-ups; there are many more but they are things for us to work on and hopefully, slowly and surely, they will fade in her memory; enough for her to let go and feel the love we have for her in our hearts.

Up until now, everything I have done with Shy has been done very slowly and quietly but to get her more used to being close to my legs, maybe it will help her if I act more normal and make a bit more noise when I am walking with her. So I start to drag and clump my feet to try to get her used to the noise, hoping she will realise there is nothing to be afraid of and just learn to ignore it. She leaps all over the place when I first start to do it, it makes me feel very guilty, but after a while, she starts to settle; it's beginning to work!

I am going to teach her to sit while at heel, so tit-bits at the ready, I ask for a 'sit'. She is very tense at first – she won't allow me to press on her back to get her into the sitting position. It has got to come from her, in her own time and sure enough, after several attempts she sits. She cannot take any tit-bits from me as she is too up-tight and eating is the last thing on her mind. So instead, I give her loads of praise and ask her to heel and we carry on walking; I then ask for another 'sit' – this time it doesn't take as long – so loads more praise and then another little walk. Again, I ask for a 'sit' and this time it's almost instant so we finish on that good note; She couldn't have done better and happily, we both go back into the house. No hesitation from Shy this time. I am able to tell John all about our successful lesson and Shy is able to chill out with Sheba.

Shy is starting to accept John a bit more. He is able to stroke her now and again but she has a deep-rooted fear of men and it will not be a quick fix. We are lucky that she is accepting me as her human friend and Sheba as her doggy friend. Between the two of us I am sure we will enable her to accept John and then maybe other people as well.

Well Sunday arrives: has it only been a week since Shy came to live with us? It feels like she has been with us forever and I cannot imagine life without her now; she has made our family complete.

We start the new week on a good note with Shy being clean again through the night. I don't think it is just luck now, I feel she is well on the way to being house trained. Daniel, one of our sons, calls to see us; Shy dives for her basket and stays there the whole of the time he is with us, I tell Daniel to ignore her and not to touch her. "Just let her get used to seeing you, there is plenty of time for you to get to know her." He does as I ask; Shy curls herself up tightly in the corner of her basket, doing her invisible dog routine again; she doesn't want to be seen and she certainly doesn't want to be touched. I can't help feeling so sorry for the little girl.

After Daniel has gone, Shy relaxes a little; she slowly creeps out of her basket and comes into the lounge to see us, her eyes shooting everywhere, checking out the room to make sure Daniel is not about to jump out at her. It must be awful, living on the edge like that her nerves must be shredded.

Because of her ordeal, I take both dogs out to play, thinking to myself how lucky we are with the weather. We've been able to get outside every day this week, which has really been a big help with Shy's training. I feel sure that if we had been able to give Shy a magic pill to help her overcome her problems, it wouldn't have done her as much good as being able to breathe the lovely fresh air, feel the soft grass under her paws and learn to play with her new best friend Sheba. Life is getting better for Shy.

Shy goes up to John for the first time today; it's only for a split second but she does it of her own free will and that is a giant step for her. John is so pleased. I know he would like to get a lot closer to Shy but the time is not quite right yet, if we try to rush her now, we might spoil the things we have already achieved; it will happen for John, I am sure.

Reflecting on our first week with Shy, I truly feel very happy. She has come so far and has given me so much to look forward to. I have always enjoyed training dogs; it's such a buzz when they learn something for the first time and I feel sure that Shy gets just as much from it as I do, she seems eager to learn and is certainly bright. Once she gets over her nervousness, I think there will be nothing she can't do; all I need to do is put the fun back into the dog.

A New Week Dawns

Another clean and quiet night. Shy is doing so well, I keep thinking it can't last; it seems too good to be true. I know when we have adopted dogs in the past we seem to get a honeymoon period where they don't put a paw wrong, usually about two weeks, and then the true dog arrives. Maybe this will happen to Shy – I hope not, but at least we won't be surprised, having had it happen in the past.

More heelwork planned for today but for a change, I think I will take her onto the front lawn where she will be able to see more things going on, like people walking past and cars going by. Sure enough, she is a lot more edgy. Although I feel sorry for her, I know she needs to experience many different things. It's not a busy lane but it is enough for her to cope with.

The rest of the day is spent mostly in the house. She is really bonding well with me now, and follows me everywhere; I know she is doing it because she is still very insecure but whatever the reason, there is a special friendship developing between us, something I am sure she has never had in the whole of her life. If she learns to really trust me, our future together looks very bright.

John is able to stroke her more, something I know he has really wanted to do but the timing has to be right. We notice that her collar is getting tighter, so we let it off a couple of holes; she must be putting on a bit of weight which can only be a good sign, as she is quite thin and needs to gain a little.

All in all the day goes well, apart from Shy being sick. I don't know what brought that on but apart from being quiet, she seems fine well it doesn't stop her from eating, she is a true Labrador were food is concerned.

I think Shy must have been feeling off yesterday because today she is dashing around the garden like a wild thing. I have never seen her act like this before and it is a delight to watch, maybe the true dog is starting to appear. I do have to be careful though, as Caroline has brought Buffy with her and unfortunately, Buffy still really dislikes Shy. I feel sure in time she will get over it but for the moment, I have to make sure they are kept apart. Shy is very scared of her and keeps out of her way but Buffy takes every chance she gets to attack her so I have to keep my wits about me.

When Buffy has gone home, Shy settles and is a lot less jumpy. While we are walking in the garden, she starts to come and touch my hand with her nose. I'm not sure why she is doing this, maybe she is just checking that I am still around but whatever the reason, it is a lovely sensation, a real connection. She really has got used to her name and most of the time comes when I call her; she is after all, a very bright little girl.

Every morning I go down the field to check on my horses and Sheba always comes too. I call her my little helper, as she collects the horse's rubber feeding bowls when they've finished their food, returns them to the barn, and drops them by the feed bins ready for the next day. She also makes sure none of the horses escape if I happen to leave one of the doors open when I am carrying several items at once such as rugs, brushes, combs etc., and find it difficult to shut the door. I haven't had to teach Sheba to do these things, she just wants to help, and she is such a clever girl. When we have finished our chores, we always go for a lovely walk across the field. We have a thirteen-acre field, which we have named Hoof beats, as we only keep horses the name seems to suit. A canal runs along one side of the field and a railway track along the other; there is an overflow from the canal so there is always water flowing in a purpose-made ditch across the field, enabling Sheba to have a paddle or swim if the water is running deeply enough. She loves that; she's always been a water babe and takes great delight in jumping and splashing around. There is a little footbridge crossing over the stream where I can stand and watch her do her stunts; she always makes me laugh.

As I watch her perform this morning, I can't help thinking how lovely it would be to be able to bring Shy to the field and watch her learn to play. Will she be a water babe? I doubt if she's ever been allowed to play around in water in the awful conditions she came from and I'm sure the dogs would have such a lot of fun playing and exploring the field together.

Sheba and I walk to the field this morning; sometimes we go in the car and sometimes we walk. While we are walking home, I start thinking how we can get Shy to the field. It is too far for her to walk just yet; she needs a lot more heelwork lessons before I think she will be ready. Could we get her into the car or would that frighten her too much? Maybe we should work on getting her in and out of the car first and if she manages that, there will be no reason why she cannot come to the field with us. I'll see what John thinks.

John also thinks it's a good idea to get her used to getting into the car but how can we do it without frightening her? John comes up with a great idea, suggesting we park the car on the front lawn, open the tailgate, and leave the dogs to jump in and out if they want to. We know Sheba will because she is quite inquisitive, it's very doubtful though if Shy will follow suit but it's worth a try.

Big Steps

October Car in position, tailgate open, we let the dogs onto the front lawn; we take to our seats and sit and watch. Sheba is looking a bit puzzled, as this is all new to her; she circles around the car a few times and then she jump in.

"Great, Sheba has done exactly what we want her to do." John says "I think it may be weeks before we get to see Shy doing that."

The words are hardly out of his mouth when Shy jumps into the car. We just look at each other and laugh; neither of us can believe what we have just seen. The dogs jump in and out several times, they are playing, and they are having fun.

We let them play for some time: it is fun for us too and we are in no hurry to end it. I think I'll go and add to the fun by playing ball with them. I throw the ball a few times for Sheba to fetch – Shy just looks on. I then roll it on the ground just past Shy and she looks puzzled; I go and fetch the ball and slowly roll it past her again. This time she goes up to it and sniffs it with her nose and as she does, it moves a little. She sniffs it again and it rolls a bit more. Shy reaches out for it and puts her mouth around the ball, she lifts up her head and the ball drops out; again, I roll it towards her. She picks it up and holds it in her mouth a little longer this time, she is learning.

I sit down on the tailgate of the car and then call Shy to me; as I do, I tap the floor of the car as I had done to get her into her basket for the first time. Much to my surprise, she comes over and jumps in. Wow, I didn't expect that. What a day – talk about big steps – I think Shy has taken giant ones today; taking her to the field appears to be a lot closer. So if I can get her into the car tomorrow morning, she will come with Sheba and me to the field.

John is going to come with us this morning if we manage to get Shy into the car. He drives the car off the front lawn and parks it on the drive. As we have no gates to close, he backs the car as close as he can to the small gate that leads into the garden where the dogs will be coming from. I know I can't have Shy on the lead as this will frighten her, so our biggest worry is that she might make a run for it; I only hope she will remember the fun she had yesterday and fingers crossed, she will follow Sheba into the car.

John stands by the drive exit just in case there is a problem; and I open the gate that leads from the garden. Then I ask Sheba to jump into the car, which she does, I take my hand off Shy's collar and let her go and there is no hesitation, she jumps straight in. I close the car door and breathe a sigh of relief; first obstacle over. John gets in and we make our way to the field; as it is only a short drive, it's the perfect distance for Shy's first trip.

Safely inside the field, we open the car door and Sheba jumps straight out, closely followed by Shy. You can see the surprise on Shy's face, she hasn't a clue where she is; it's another world for her to explore.

Up until now, I've been feeling confident that Shy will follow me as she has done in her heelwork lessons, but with all the other things for her to see, I'm not feeling quite so confident now. The field is a big space, thirteen acres in all; if she takes it into her head to run off, we will never be able to catch her. But we have got Sheba, so I hope Shy will follow her lead and we will be able to relax and enjoy the walk.

Shy is finding it strange to have John walking with us. She is giving him a very wide birth, continually circling around us, not getting too close but not going too far away either. We walk the whole of the field, which must seem enormous to Shy; she's edgy at times and a little jumpy but overall, we think she is really enjoying herself. She even has a little paddle when she sees Sheba splashing about in the stream; I am sure some of Sheba's splashes are aimed at Shy who hasn't got the hang of the water game yet she's not quite sure about this getting wet thing and spends most of the time watching from dry land.

We are wondering how Shy will react when she first meets our horses – and how the horses will react to her. They can sometimes be very skittish when meeting a new dog, so we will have to be careful; John goes and strokes one of the horses while Shy stays with me looking on. Then I walk up to the horse with Shy following and there is no reaction from either side. The other horses carry on grazing, occasionally lifting their heads just to check who the new kid on the block is but apart from that, she is accepted. Shy shows no fear at all which is quite surprising and I can only think no horse had ever harmed her, so she has nothing to worry about; in fact, she seems very relaxed when she is around them.

It would be lovely to think that one day she will be as relaxed around people, but with an animal as traumatised as this, I don't think she'll ever be able to completely let it all go so the best we can hope for is that she will improve. However, if we can carry on introducing her to new and exciting things, her remaining life should be a much happier place.

We have no trouble getting the dogs in the car to go home and neither of us can quite believe how well things have gone. All being well, she will be able to come to the field with Sheba and me every morning from now on, so we are both in a very happy mood. Later in the day I go into the kitchen to start lunch, only to find Shy has eaten our lovely tiger loaf.

"Great way to repay us"! I say jokingly to her, the walk must have made her extra hungry.

This morning my spirits are still on a high, so I am going to take the dogs to the field on my own; though a lot depends on whether I can get both of them into the car; Shy is a little apprehensive but when I sit on the tail gate and tap the floor, she again jumps in. I'm very relieved when both dogs are safely in the car and off we go to the field. As I'm driving, I chat happily to the dogs, telling them how well they are doing, and how proud I am of them; I don't know whether they can understand but they must know I am in a good mood from the tone of my voice.

There's no problem with getting them out, in fact when I open the car door both dogs leap out with great enthusiasm. (Mental note to self – must work on that, as it could be a problem if we hadn't been in such a safe place). For the moment, I am just pleased that Shy looks so happy to be free; I check the horses and take the dogs a walk around the field and everything goes great.; Shy is looking and acting more like a dog all the time, she is still very clingy with me but it's early days after all.

There is a fenced off portion in the field that I keep to school the horses on, which is flat and the grass is nice and short. I find it's the perfect place to practice heelwork and obedience lessons with Sheba, so this morning I am going to do some work with her and let Shy watch and hopefully, learn.

We practise heelwork on and off the lead and finish with some recalls. When it's Shy's turn, I pop her lead on and try doing some heelwork with her but she gets very frightened – she knows she can't get away and that scares her.

O.K, we will do it all off the lead; after all, there's no rush; it is still very early days.

When Shy gets worried she can't be tempted with titbits, so I know, she has to follow me because she wants to, not just for a treat. We don't do too much but what we do impresses me; she quickly gets the idea and stays close by my side. It helps a lot that she is still very clingy to me and I will be able to use this to help her learn.

There is no trouble getting both dogs back into the car, and we are able to go home feeling tired but good about what we have achieved. John looks relieved when we arrive home and it's great to sit down with a cup of coffee and tell him all about what we have been doing.

Shy has always tended to lick my arms and hands when I am sitting down; I think it must be a nervous thing, or it might be a hangover from washing her puppies. If so she must have had the cleanest puppies in the land, I know my arms and hands have never felt cleaner. Tonight she goes over and licks John's hand for the first time, just for a moment but it is lovely to see; she is learning to trust John.

Shy's First Meeting with Strangers

Friends of ours, Janet and her daughter Rebecca, keep their horse Swampy on our field and every weekend they come to visit him. He came to us many years ago to be broken in as a youngster; at the time, my friend and I were breaking in young horses for their owners to ride.

When Swampy was ready to go home, it was decided he would stay at the field because he seemed very relaxed and comfortable in his surroundings; he is now in his twenties and I can't imagine the field without Swampy on it. He's a very large, impressive looking black and white cob; the sort that would have been used to pull a plough years ago and although large in stature, he is a gentle giant. We have pictures of Niki and Liam, two of our grandchildren sitting on him when they were very young (he is that good). He was given the name Swampy after Janet's husband saved him from drowning when he got stuck in a muddy pond as a foal. Of course, they had a very strong affection for the foal after that, and as Rebecca was showing a real interest in horses and taking riding lessons at the time, they decided to buy him.

Knowing that Janet and Rebecca are coming to the field today, I am not sure how Shy will react to seeing them for the first time. However, I have told Janet all about Shy so she knows it will be best if they just ignore the dog when they first meet her.

Sure enough when Shy lays eyes on the pair, she immediately runs quite a distance away. Sheba goes up and greets them as Shy looks on; while talking to Janet, I am watching Shy out of the corner of my eye. She seems to be curious and starts to edge a little closer; I know she is not happy to be so far away from me but her nerves have got the better of her.

We leave the pair to see to their horse and go for our walk. The relief in Shy's eyes is very noticeable as she pushes herself even closer to my leg, hardly leaving my side the whole of the walk.

When our walk is over, we meet up again with Janet and Rebecca but as we walk back to the car, Shy circles around and around us; there is no way she is going to come too close. Rebecca remarks on what lovely movement she has and I'm thinking the same; she is a nice looking dog, I guess that is one of the reasons they bred from her.

Shy won't jump into the car with the pair standing close by; she probably thinks it's a trap and that once inside the car she won't be able to escape. However, when they are out of sight, Shy immediately jumps into the car with Sheba. I am very relieved, as I did not fancy picking her up, she's not the heaviest of dogs but I think I would have struggled.

Well, Shy has had her first meeting with strangers and because we were in the field, she wasn't able run and hide in her basket. I think overall, she coped very well. It is good she has bonded so well with me as it means that I'm her safety net and of course, Sheba is her confidence booster. I think between us we will be able to help this little girl come to grips with and conquer the fears she has now.

John is allowed to stroke her again – I say allowed, because it has to come from her and be on her terms; we know the inevitable will happen if we try to rush things, she'll just run away and hide. She will let us know when she feels the time is right and as I have said before, listen and your little friend will talk to you.

Sunday arrives; it has been just two weeks since we brought Shy home and it's hard to believe how far she has come in such a short time. She meets Janet and Rebecca again today, and doesn't run quite so far away but still keeps a safe distance. It might take months before she gets comfortable with them around but that doesn't matter – as long as she keeps her trust in me, that's all we can wish for at the moment.

I have been cleaning Shy's ears out every two days; the Dogs Trust advised us to take her to the vet after two weeks to have her ears checked. However I don't feel any pain in her ears anymore so I've decided not to take her to the vets, as I think it could be too problematic for her to cope with; of course, if I do feel she is starting to get pain again, I won't hesitate to take her.

Well the week has finished on a good note – Shy is turning out to be a real pleasure to own – She has no problem in letting me handle her and has accepted her new name, returning to me whenever I call to her. I always look forward to every new day with her.

The Dog Arrives

The beginning of a new week – how time flies – we are entering our third week with Shy. Sheba is limping; she seems to have hurt her front paw so we will only be doing a gentle walk today and I will see how she is later.

John decides to come to the field with us and he is impressed to see how Shy has improved. It is more noticeable to him as he doesn't come to the field every day and he feels she has really moved on; I know she is getting better but it's always nice to hear it from someone else. We don't stay down the field very long because of Sheba's leg but I am able to show John how Shy's heel work is coming on. I don't think he quite believes what he is seeing.

John parks the car on the drive when we arrive home and opens the rear door to let out the dogs; unfortunately, he doesn't notice that a cat is walking past but Sheba does; she shoots out of the car (very unaware of her bad leg) and chases after the cat, followed closely by Shy. We are very lucky no cars were driving past, or I think there could have been a nasty accident. I run out onto the road and call to them and Sheba reluctantly comes back with Shy in tow. Phew, that was too close for comfort but the rest of the day goes by with no further problems.

With the magic two weeks being up, it's no surprise to me when I open the kitchen door this morning to find towels, toys, gloves, trainers, leads and even a tape measure chewed up and lying on the floor. Sheba does not know where to look. I think she is expecting to get the blame but I know who the culprit is; the innocent little dog now lying quite happily curled up in her basket.

There is no way I can be mad at her, in fact it's good to see she is being more normal, letting go and acting more like a dog, just as you would expect to find if she had been a puppy, I doubt if she's ever been able to display these sort of actions being caged. It must feel very good for her to be able to release some of her tensions. I do make a mental note however, to make sure I put everything out of her reach tonight; all except dog toys that is.

I feel I can increase the level of her training now that her confidence is getting better. She gives me the impression of being very eager to learn, reminding me of a sponge, wanting to absorb as much and as quickly as she can, trying to catch up on all that she has missed. She is a very bright little girl and I feel she could have gone far under different circumstances.

Teaching her more things might be the key to a happier, more confident dog, allowing her to experience the challenge of learning and the satisfaction of getting it right. As long as it doesn't start to worry her, I think this is the way to go.

Meeting More People

Mathew our son and his wife Tracey, pay us a visit and of course, they want to meet Shy. They themselves have a Labrador dog, a big brute of a dog called Jinx. They haven't brought him with them and I am pleased about that, as Shy is not ready yet. Jinx has a lovely temperament but he is quite an animal to look at, being about three times the size of Shy and black in colour; he could have looked very frightening to her.

Shy never leaves her basket the whole of the time they are with us but she doesn't run away either, she just watches their every move. Tracey tries talking to her, but she is having none of it, and she does her normal trick of pushing herself tightly into the corner of her basket to try to make herself become invisible. Tracey cannot believe how nervous she is; she has never seen a dog so traumatised before but she has never been in contact with a puppy farm dog. The damage that can be done, not just physically but also mentally, is hard for any caring human to understand. Jinx was bought as a puppy from a loving home; he hasn't any hang-ups, and he's just a happy go lucky dog – the sort of dog Shy should have been.

Although Tracey found Shy to be very scared and frightened, John and I both know she has made great steps since we have had her. We see the dog that other people can't see; the little dog that's starting to trust, starting to play, starting to learn. Maybe we will be the only people to see the real Shy – maybe she will never be able to trust others; all I know is that she must see us as being very special to allow us to share her life; it's a two-way thing, she is very special to us too.

Shy's Brief Encounter with Buffy

Shy meets Buffy twice today, by accident. I am not aware Buffy is in the garden and she surprises Shy by racing up to her as greyhounds do. Shy just stands frozen to the spot as Buffy jumps around her but Caroline sees what is happening and calls Buffy to her. Shy disappears into the house, a little shaken but not hurt; I am pleased that Buffy was not as nasty to Shy as she had been at their last meeting.

Later in the day, it happens all over again, but this time Buffy is bossier, trying to let Shy know she is in charge. I can see what is happening and am able to send Buffy off with a flea in her ear; I'm not going to let her frighten Shy again; after all, I want Shy to be able to relax in her own garden and not be afraid in case Buffy pounces. As Buffy comes most days, I guess she thinks it is her territory but she has to learn that Shy lives here now and she must accept her; I feel she will in time but we must try to make it as amicable as possible.

Big steps though – Shy lets Caroline stroke her while she is lying in her basket. I can't say she looks very comfortable with the experience but she doesn't growl or try to run away.

We have apple trees and this year we have a bumper crop; Sheba loves to eat any apples that fall to the ground but its obvious Shy has never seen an apple in her life before. She seems fascinated as she sits and watches Sheba munching away, it takes a while for her to realise that they are yummy to eat but when she does, there is no stopping her. I am forever trying to pick up the apples before the dogs find them and make pigs of themselves, but I'm afraid I'm fighting a losing battle.

Whether apples are the cause or it was the events of the day, I don't know but Shy goes to the toilet in the back porch twice today, something she hasn't done for quite a while; I must remember to open the door faster after she has eaten her tea in future.

Friday is a quiet day, Shy did some good heelwork in the field and she's getting less jumpy and is learning to sit before she has her meals. This takes a lot of control on her part, as food must have been the main event in her old life. Maybe the most dominant dog ate first and the rest had the scraps. I am only surmising this as I don't know but I can see with my own eyes the way she attacks her food, frantically looking all about and jumping at any little noise or movement around her. I always feed her out in the porch so she can be on her own, not having to worry that Sheba may pinch her dinner – not that Sheba could since Shy eats so fast, there would only ever be an empty dish for Sheba to lick.

I enjoy painting and whenever I go into the room where I do my painting, Shy follows me and jumps onto the spare bed in there. She lies down, lets out a deep sigh, and then drifts off to sleep, never moving until she hears me getting up to leave. She goes into a very relaxed state; I think she must be picking up on the way I feel when I am painting. John always says painting is the only thing I do that really relaxes me and he's always encouraged me to do it; If that's the case, both Shy and I must be in tune with one another.

PART THREE

The Next Stage

Sharing Traits

The more I study Shy's behaviour, the more our little granddaughter Ellie springs to mind. She has always been a bit of a worry to us because although she is seven years old, she has never been able to show any affection towards us – her shyness is extreme. Her little brother James on the other hand, is quite the opposite, outgoing and very bright; Ellie relies on him a lot, even though she is nearly three years older.

Ellie is perfectly all right with her parents but finds it hard to talk to anyone else. I find this hurtful, as I miss the cuddles and closeness you can expect to get from your grandchildren, the same sort of relationship we have with our other grandchildren; she is a real puzzle to us.

Concern has been shown at school, as they too are worried about her and the family has had to attend several meetings to try to find the underlying cause of Ellie's problem but nothing has seemed to help.

The only way I'm able to make any headway with her, is to make a game of it and pretend I have stolen her tongue and as long as I have it, she can't speak. Naturally telling anyone not to do something will make them want to do it and it seems to work.

"I can talk," She shouts, and I shake my head and say, "not while I've got your tongue".

We play this game until I pretend to give her tongue back. By this time, she starts to forget herself and begins to talk a little – her sense of humour coming to the surface. She can see the twinkle in my eye and realises we are just having fun so she starts to relax and comes out of her shell. It's very short-lived though, as she dives back into her little hidey-hole whenever she feels she can't cope but I find this game very useful and it always seems to get good results when everything else seems to fail. Things are slowly starting to happen but it is just a small drop in a very large ocean.

One day I was half watching and half listening to a television program, when I heard a woman talking about some dogs they have in America that go to schools to help children who have various problems. They particularly seemed to help children who had been diagnosed with Selective Mutism. I was all ears at that point as it seemed to make sense to me that that's what Ellie has; we knew she could talk, but only when she wanted to. I told John and he went on the internet and looked up the symptoms of Selective Mutism. Sure enough, everything seemed to fit into place and at last, we had something to work on. I felt a lot happier, as it wasn't us she didn't like – she has a problem and problems can be solved. At last, we had something to work on.

I phoned our son Adam to let him know what we'd found out and amazingly, Ellie had just been diagnosed with Selective Mutism; it seemed we'd all got there at the same time. Well, better late than never.

You might wonder why I am talking about Ellie's problems and how does this tie in with Shy? Well as I said, when I watch Shy I see similarities. Shy's problems were bought on by abuse I know; Ellie's weren't but like Shy, Ellie shuts herself off and disappears into her own little world, much the same as Shy does when she can't cope with things. Ellie finds it difficult to talk; it's as if she doesn't want to draw attention to herself while Shy seems afraid to bark, which I presume is a type of talking in the dog world and they both suffer from extreme shyness.

With this in mind, I wonder if the little dog can help Ellie. I know she loves all kinds of animals and she has always been very fond of Sheba so maybe the pair could help each other get over their extreme shyness. I really hope so.

Meeting the Little People

We look after our two little grandchildren every other Saturday for a few hours and this Saturday they are due to come to us. It was their turn to come to us a couple of weeks ago but because we'd only had Shy a week at that time, we thought it would be too much for the little dog to cope with. After all, we don't even know if she's ever had any contact with children, and children can be very noisy, running around and slamming doors etc.

We'll keep Shy in the kitchen while they are with us and we're going to tell the children not to go in there until she has been with us longer; they're good kids and we know they'll listen and do as they are told.

Two very excited children arrive with their mother this morning. They've already been told we have a new dog and they just can't wait to see her. I sit down with the lively, excitable pair and explain to them all about poor Shy's past. I can see Ellie is taking it all in; she may not talk very much but she understands. She looks deep in thought.

Then I say, "Shy is very much like you Ellie, she is very Shy. That's why we gave her that name. You know what it's like to be so shy, it's not nice is it?"

I can almost read her mind; her little eyes light up and it's as if she has found someone else who has the same problem as she has; she almost looks relieved she isn't on her own anymore. "So can I rely on the two of you to treat her nicely? Will you try to be a lot quieter this week, because noise really frightens her and you mustn't go into the kitchen, because that will really scare her." I know they are disappointed but they promise to be good.

Shy does not leave her basket the whole of the morning; she just lies there listening to all the strange noises. I only let Sheba out of the kitchen to say hello to the children and then put her back to keep Shy company. The children are good, they keep going to the kitchen door to look through the glass to hopefully catch sight of Shy and every now and again, we hear squeals of delight as they catch a glimpse of her. I am sure in their little way, they really feel sorry for her and we can hear them chatting amongst themselves. Yes, Ellie is chatting – more than we have ever heard – and all they seem to talk about is Shy; they even draw some pictures of her to show their mum and dad.

I hope that when they come to visit next time they'll be able to go and see Shy. I can only see good things coming from this; maybe Shy will be able to help Ellie and maybe, Ellie can help Shy.

Adjusting to Normal Life

The next few days pass by without many hitches; life is beginning to take on a routine, and Shy is fitting very nicely into it. She is getting better around Janet and Rebecca, not so jumpy but always keeping a safe distance. Around the horses she is still very comfortable and shows no fear of them, quite happily walking around their legs and letting them sniff her face and back. It is amazing how the sheer size of the horses does not seem to worry her; she appears to have complete trust in them and them in her.

John and I are going to the field this afternoon to pick blackberries and rosehips, and of course, the dogs are coming too; the blackberries are for us (yummy blackberry and apple pie for tea) and the rosehips are for the horses. They are a good sauce of biotin and I slowly bake and grind them up to put in their feed, which is good for their hooves. It takes us quite a while, there's no quick way to pick berries; the dogs have plenty of time to play and do their own thing, leaving us to do all the work.

Shy's heelwork is coming on well. I've taken to carrying the lead in my hand, for her to get used to me holding it and then when we finish our lesson, I throw it for her to chase. I'm trying to make the lesson fun for her and it seems to be working.

I notice that when I wear a change of clothes, Shy gets very nervous. I am not sure if she recognises me at first; the people who have been around her in the past, have probably always been in overalls and welly boots and she finds it difficult to accept me in anything different. I do wear wellies and old trousers when I go down the field but I am hoping in time she'll be able to accept me in something different.

Sometimes she gets nervous when I go to put the lead on her, and won't let me catch her but it's never long before she comes back and gives herself up; I think she's learning that

I'm not going to hurt her. Today I am going to take her for a little walk up the lane as I want to see how she will react if any cars pass us; she's edgy but overall not too bad.

I am very pleased with how Shy behaved yesterday, so I'm taking her a little further this morning. There's a village hall not too far from where we live with a car park. As there are hardly ever any cars parked there, it makes the perfect place to take Shy. We walk several times around the car park and she copes well, until we meet a man and it takes all my strength to hold on to her until he passes by.

Four weeks pass and overall, I think Shy is doing extremely well. She is not skidding around the laminated floor so much, which can only mean her nerves are getting a little better; her heelwork on and off the lead is coming on well; she's learning to play and is getting more comfortable with her new life. She's going to John more and doesn't jump so much when he walks past her. She's still glued to my leg but give it time.

If the next four weeks go as well as the first four we will be more than happy. I think she has achieved a lot in what is only a very short time and I'm looking forward to the challenges that lie ahead; life will never be dull while Shy is around.

Starting to Explore

I think I'll try and find one of Sheba's old balls to see if Shy will show any interest in running after it. After searching through Sheba's toy box I come across one that she hasn't played with for a long time. I think she has forgotten all about it but of course, as soon as she spots the old forgotten ball, she gets very excited and rushes to the door knowing we are about to play a game; out in the garden, I throw the ball and she rushes off to bring it back to me, she always enjoys this game.

Shy stands watching Sheba do all the work and she seems to be weighing up the situation; then it clicks and she starts to run after the ball. Sheba can run much faster than Shy and always reaches the ball first so if I'm going to teach Shy to play ball, I know Sheba can't be on the scene so after we have been playing for a while, I put Sheba back into the house so I can spend some time alone with Shy.

Shy really has a great time chasing the ball and she looks very proud of herself when she bounds back to me with it in her mouth. I can't help smiling as she runs towards me – she looks like she is grinning from ear to ear. The problem I have is getting the ball off her; she doesn't like letting it go and hasn't quite got the hang of the game yet. I throw; she fetches and gives it back to me. But she'll learn.

We are still having problems with Buffy who has not come to accept Shy yet. It is a shame as she's always got on well with Sheba but maybe she's a little jealous; after all Sheba has always been her friend so maybe she's finding it hard to share her.

I take Shy for another little walk on her own but instead of going the same way as before, I take her in the opposite direction, where there are more houses and more things for her to get used to. Two cars pass us from behind, which is always a little scarier for dogs; I can't say Shy enjoys the experience but she copes well.

We feel it's time to put Shy's basket into the kitchen proper; not too close to Sheba's basket but close enough for them to see each other. However it doesn't work, as Shy won't get into her basket – it's too soon – so we put it back into the little room adjoining the kitchen and she jumps straight in.

Another Bad Day with Buffy

The dogs and I have just returned from the field and we're going through the gate into the back garden, when Buffy charges at Shy. She really means it this time; she is out for a fight. I happen to be holding an empty plastic bag in my hand that had held treats for the horses, so as Buffy gets level with us, I shout angrily and slam the bag down on her back, making a loud noise. Buffy stops in her tracks and I don't think she realises where the noise has come from; she may even think Shy has made it. Whatever it is it does the trick, as Buffy turns tail and runs away. In the following days Buffy leaves Shy alone and at last they seem to have started to respect one another; Shy is still very wary but we seem to be going in the right direction.

One of our walks in the field nearly turns out badly when Shy decides to take it into her head to push through the hedge to get onto the canal towpath. It's a lovely morning and I'm in a little world of my own as I follow the two dogs across the field; being deep in thought, I miss seeing Shy disappear through the hedge and it's only when I see Sheba behaving strangely, running up and down along our side of the hedge, that I realise something is wrong. I quickly look around for Shy but she's nowhere to be seen and my heart sinks. She must be on the towpath and I know if she meets anyone, she will panic and make a run for it. How can I get her back? I can't push through the hedge it's much too thick, so all I can do is keep shouting her name. I know roughly where she is as Sheba is running up and down keeping up with her but staying on our side of the hedge. Shy wants to come back but she can't remember where she'd pushed through. Then luckily, Sheba finds the hole in the hedge and puts her head through it. For one awful moment, I think she is going through as well, but no, being such a clever dog she is showing Shy the way back and sure enough, the next thing I see is Shy pushing her way back into the field – what a relief!

I give both dog's loads and loads of praise and some treats that I always carry in my pocket. I can't be mad with Shy as she doesn't know the field has boundaries; if I look on the positive side, she is getting braver and learning how to explore, and the bonus is she came back. She wanted to be with us – what more can I wish for?

Meeting Lucky

Daniel pops in to see us again and this time he brings Lucky his dog with him. Lucky is also a rescue dog, re-homed from a rescue centre a few years earlier; he's a collie cross and came with a bit of a reputation as a dog that had been known to bite but even knowing this, Daniel and Michelle fell in love with him and adopted him. I always found this a bit strange, as they'd turned down the chance to own Sheba because they thought she looked too frightening and in her place, chose to take on a dog that was known to bite. He obviously sold himself to them. He was a bit snappy at first but soon settled and has turned into a lovely animal; it just goes to show that we all see different things in different animals and if we trust our instincts things usually turn out right.

I'm playing in the garden with the dogs when Daniel and Lucky arrive. Sheba likes Lucky and always enjoys his visits but I'm not sure how Shy will react, especially after all the problems we've had with Buffy lately; I'm feeling very concerned. Fortunately, Lucky seems more interested in playing with his friend Sheba; after introducing himself by sniffing Shy, he leaves her alone.

Shy doesn't seem too worried, she must have picked up on Lucky's vibes and knows he isn't going to hurt her; she's more worried about Daniel and won't go close to him. Even seeing her like this, Daniel says how much she has improved since the last time he saw her and how lovely it is to see her running about and not cowering in her basket. He can see she is starting to act more like a dog and I'm happy to hear this as it shows that all the work we've been doing is beginning to pay off.

Not far from our house, there's a very quiet dead-end lane that leads nowhere – the perfect place to take Shy for a longer walk. It's a lovely little lane with hardly any houses and I've often walked the horses up and down it if they needed gentle exercise while convalescing at home. You hardly meet any people or cars and on a good day, you meet nothing.

Shy is walking quite nicely on the lead now so I think it'll do her good to walk a bit further to show her more of the area where she now lives; we pass the village hall where we have stopped before and she pulls across, expecting to go into the car park. Clever girl I think, there's nothing wrong with your memory. She hesitates as she realises we're not stopping but carrying on, this is something new again and she is unsure but she listens to me and carries on walking. We go as far as we can along the lane and then turn around and head for home. I'm very pleased with how she is coping; yes she's a bit jumpy, I expect that – but she is listening to me and heeling very nicely. Several cars pass us on the way back, more than usual, but they don't seem to frighten her as much as people do. I'm sure if she realises there's a person in the car, it might be a different matter, but luckily, she doesn't.

When we get home, I take her into the garden to play ball with her. I've decided to play with two balls, so when she brings one back, I throw the other one straight away, hoping she'll drop the first and chase after the second. She soon gets the hang of this and it's not long before she's quite happily dropping one ball for me to pick up, while she chases after the other one. The game goes well and I think it won't long before we can play with just one ball for her to fetch and bring back, for me to throw again.

This morning Shy got out onto the canal towpath again. I don't understand what the attraction is; the only good thing is that she came back very quickly when she found the gap in the hedge and doesn't need Sheba's help this time. At least I can see where she escaped and I'm able to block the hole but as the hedges are now getting thinner, I'll have to be extra vigilant, as I would hate this to become a habit. We finish the walk with her doing some great heelwork, the best yet, so all is forgiven.

The weather is getting worse; the lovely dry days we had when we first brought Shy home have been replaced with wet, miserable conditions; the field is getting very muddy and the dogs look more like bog monsters every day. Because the weather is so awful, the dogs aren't coming to the field with me so much now so I try and make it up to them by taking them in the garden when the rain stops. We play ball and try to have a little fun; small consolation, I know.

We have a rare rain free day today, so the dogs come with me to the field and we have a lovely walk but have to be careful where we go as some parts of the field are very muddy. On our way back to the car, I spot Janet with her husband Ray in the field. As it's not Janet's normal day, I am surprised to see them and Sheba rushes up to greet them both. However, Shy is starting to look very nervous as she hasn't met Ray before so I decide not to hang around and after shouting "Hello" I walk back towards the car, which is parked by the gate.

As I'm walking, I notice that a couple of the plastic electric fence posts are leaning, so I go across to push them deeper into the ground. For a moment, I take my eyes off the dogs that are walking slightly ahead of me. Suddenly I hear Ray shout and I look up to see that Janet and Ray have been walking behind us; they're not that close but near enough to frighten Shy. I look round but I can only see Sheba.

"She's out on the road!" Ray shouts. He'd seen her push through the hedge by the gate – I rush towards it, shouting her name as loud as I can and when I get there, she's just the other side of it. She looks as relieved to see me as I am to see her and doesn't hesitate to return to the field when I open the gate. Janet and Ray look very relieved and stand well back to let me get the dogs into the car. That's another hole to block

I think to myself; my little dog is turning out to be quite an escape artist.

Stepping Out

The weather is turning much colder now and this morning the dogs have to watch impatiently as I try and scrape the ice off the car windscreen. I am obviously taking too long and they are getting increasingly agitated. "Alright" I say; "we'll walk to the field and get rid of some of your energy".

I return to the house and collect their leads and Sheba's back pack; she always carries the horses' treats for me when we walk to the field and is good at her job. I feel a bit nervous, as this will be the biggest step Shy has taken since coming to live with us; she's doing really well with her heelwork but taking both dogs out together on their leads might be a step too far. Oh well I think, if the worst comes to the worst we can always turn round and come home; I tell John we're going to walk to the field and he looks quite worried. "It's alright, I've got my phone, if there's a problem I'll call you". On that note, I confidently set off but of course, I am just putting on an act. However, there always has to be a first time to try something new and today seems to be the perfect day. It's a beautiful morning, the sort that lifts your spirits and it makes a lovely change from the dismal wet days we've had recently. I know the field will be firmer because of the frost and that will make it much nicer for the dogs. Yes, it's the perfect day to try something new.

I position Sheba so she'll be nearest to the cars and helping to shield Shy, who I keep on the inside. There are no footpaths, so when cars do pass they come very close and this must be frightening for the dogs. Sheba of course, has done this trip many times and cars don't bother her. Shy at first keeps trying to turn around and pull backwards and I have to keep encouraging her to move forward but after a while, she gets the idea and starts to keep up with Sheba.

Things are going really well until I spot a woman walking towards us with two small dogs. My heart sinks. I know Sheba doesn't get on with small dogs and if they start to bark, she'll retaliate. I visualize Shy bolting backwards with Sheba pulling forwards to get at them, with me being split down the middle. I ask Sheba to sit and then brace myself for the inevitable and the two little dogs walk past, yapping excitedly. Sheba looks on but she doesn't move an inch; I have never known her to be so good and I feel she is really trying to look after us this morning. The rest of the walk goes well but I must admit it's a relief when we reach the field and I can let the dogs loose so they can run free and enjoy themselves.

When we are ready to walk back, I am surprised to see John standing by the gate; he's come down in the car to take us home. He must have thought walking both ways would be too much for us. He's parked the car in the gateway with the tailgate open so the dogs can jump in. He calls to the dogs as we approach and they run up to the car. I watch as Sheba jumps in but Shy shoots past and runs straight out onto the road. Not again! I don't think my nerves can take much more.

John shouts to Shy but she carries on running in the direction of home and when I reach the gate, she is just about to run over the canal bridge which is about fifty metres from the field. "Shy!" I shout, as calmly as I can. She stops in her tracks, turns around, and ran back to me. I look at John and he's pale; he knows it could have been very nasty if Shy had met a car on the narrow bridge. "Looking on the bright side," I say, "at least she was heading for home".

I don't feel too well this morning, so John checks the horses for me. He doesn't take the dogs with him, so later in the day when I'm starting to feel better; I take them into the garden to play. Shy is playing a lot more with toys now and as she hasn't any of her own, she pinches Sheba's; Sheba doesn't seem to mind but we must buy Shy some of her own now she is showing an interest.

November

I'm feeling a lot better this morning so I take Shy for a walk up the lane. We have a nice walk but it's a bit spoilt by meeting a man walking towards us with two dogs. I don't think the dogs worry Shy as much as the man does but once they walk past, we are able to continue the walk quite calmly. The fear seems to be leaving her more quickly now and she doesn't seem to worry about it for so long.

When we reach home, I take her into the garden to play ball. She's just started to bring the ball back and give it to me; she really loves playing this game and it's a great way for her to release her tensions. She never seems to tire of me throwing the ball for her but I am afraid it tires me. When the game is over, we do some heel-work. I'm teaching her to walk on both sides of me, so when I walk the two dogs together, she won't always expect to be walking on the same side. I am also starting to teach her to stay; she finds this hard as she still likes to be glued to my leg but it's starting to sink in and I don't think it'll be too long before she really gets the idea.

She's getting very fussy around me when I'm sitting watching TV. After her ritual of washing my hands and arms, she tries to jump onto my lap. It's as if she really wants to but hasn't quite got the nerve to take her hind legs off the floor. I don't want to encourage her; she's too big to be a lap dog. It's a fine line between allowing her to show affection to me and letting her get into bad habits.

We've bought Shy a tug-toy all of her own and now when we go to the field, she takes it with her; Sheba has her ball and Shy has her tuggy. It seems to work because Sheba doesn't try to grab Shy's toy when I throw it, she waits for me to throw her ball.

Buffy is starting to get on better with Shy; in fact, all three of them have been seen walking around the garden together; I can't say Buffy and Shy are best friends yet but they're learning to tolerate one another and the rest will hopefully follow.

Shy is a very bouncy little dog with a lot of energy and she is really enjoying the freedom she now has to let off steam. With this in mind, I'm going make a little jump and see if she will go over it. From time to time I put up small jumps for Sheba who really enjoys the game, so she knows exactly what I'm up to when I start making the jump. There's no hesitation on her part when I shout 'OVER' to her. Shy looks on, excited but unsure; I call her to me and run with her by my side, shouting 'OVER' when we reach the jump. I step across it (well I did say it was only a small jump) but Shy runs out to the side. We do this several times until finally she jumps, whereupon I give her plenty of praise and a titbit and she is bitten by the bug; I can tell from her excitement that she's loving every minute.

I put another jump up, a bit higher this time so now she has two to jump, one after the other. Sheba finds this all too easy–she is used to much larger jumps. I position Shy and we run towards the jumps. When she lands after the first one, I shout 'ON' and point to the second jump. She runs on and clears it with ease and we finish on that very happy note.

Shy Helps Sheba Overcome Her Fears

November the fifth: I always dread that date. I'm not sure how Shy will behave when she hears all the noise; Sheba hates it and we always worry about the horses. We try to make it as safe as possible for them but that's all we can do and I hate going down to the field the morning after bonfire night in case something awful has happened to any of them. I feel very uneasy when it starts to get dark, what sort of night are we in for?

When all the bangs and squeals of the fireworks begin, John and I brace ourselves for the onset of Sheba's hysterical barking as she dashes uncontrollably around the house. This time, Sheba lets out a few little barks when she hears the first fireworks and then stops, while Shy takes no notice at all. John and I look at each other; surely, that's not it — but it is. We have the most peaceful bonfire night for a long time and to top it all the horses are fine in the morning. In this instance, Shy's calmness has rubbed off on Sheba and she has been able to help Sheba overcome her fear of fireworks.

The rest of the week goes by without any problems. Shy is still doing very well with her jumping and I make a jump in the field so she can continue having fun when we are taking our walk; she finds it confusing at first but it doesn't take her long before she follows Sheba's lead and joins her in having fun.

I take every opportunity to introduce Shy to new experiences and when I hear John using his noisy chainsaw, I put her lead on and take her past him several times. She doesn't like the experience but she trusts me enough to stay close to me and I reassure her that nothing is going to harm her.

Shy is learning some new tricks, like spinning around when I ask; she's almost got the hang of sitting up and begging but her balance isn't as good as Sheba's and she tends to topple over in her rush to take the treat from my hand.

John and I need to do some work in the field this morning and we take the dogs with us even though we know they'll come back covered in mud (they do not disappoint!). They have a great time, seemingly sorting out the muddiest parts of the field to wallow in; I'll never quite understand the fascination of mud baths but of course, I am not a dog. It's lovely to see Shy walking a lot closer to John than she's done in the past – things are still going in the right direction.

Shy has her second meeting with the children this weekend. We allow them in the kitchen this time but warn them not to touch her, as we don't know what her reaction might be if they get too close. They do their best to stay quiet but I'm sure Shy still finds it very noisy. She spends all the time they're with us in her basket; only venturing out once she's sure they've gone home. I find out on their next visit that Ellie actually stroked Shy in her basket. I was not happy to hear this but luckily, no harm was done and maybe a bond is starting to form.

After the children have gone home, John and I take the two dogs up the lane, and on the way back I hand Shy's lead to John so he can walk her home. Shy is scared at first, she has only walked on her lead with me and this is something different again. Seeing her reaction to walking with John, I decide to walk ahead with Sheba to make Shy realise that if she wants to be with me, she has to walk faster to catch me up – and she does. By the time we reach home, she's walking very nicely by John's side.

An Eventful Week

Half the week goes well but the other half isn't so good: in the good half, when we're taking the dogs out, John manages to walk with Shy up and down the lane and she is much more relaxed and less worried about him holding the lead. Shy is still behaving well when cars pass us but when she hears voices coming from the village hall, it really frightens her.

Her lessons in the garden are still going well and she's learning to go into the 'down' position when asked. She is very reluctant to do this and I think she feels vulnerable lying down unless she's in her basket; her 'safe' place.

In the not-so-good half of the week, returning from the field, I have a problem getting Shy out of the car when she spots that Buffy is in the garden; I have to resort to pulling her out.

Another day, another escape onto the towpath, but again, she comes back when she finds her own way through the hedge. When we arrive home, she sees Adam's car parked in the driveway and this frightens her so that she won't get out of the car and I have to pull her out yet again. It doesn't end there either; I can't get her into the house because she spots Adam is indoors and I have to put her lead on before she will follow me inside.

Later, when I want to take her into the garden for her toilet training, she won't get out of her basket. This time I think it's because Caroline is bobbing about in the kitchen, so again I have to put her lead on to take her out; it hasn't been the best of days but I hope it's just a hiccup.

Today I hear Shy give her first little whimper. She's waiting with Sheba to come back into the house. It's lovely to hear and I think she's finding her voice at last. She seems much more settled this week after last week's escapades and is playing more with Sheba and her toys. They have a good game of tug when they both want the same toy and she even lets out a little growl and manages to win the toy; the real dog is starting to appear.

Shy's Confidence Is Growing

I'm still not taking the dogs to the field much because of the weather but spend more time doing lessons with Shy in the garden; her heelwork is becoming excellent. Although I've always tried to teach my dogs to do good heel-work, Shy is turning out to be the best; she walks to heel both on and off the lead and always turns her head to look into my eyes. I've never managed to get any of my other dogs to do this; they've all heeled well but she always gives me her full attention and the best of it is she really wants to. The only downside is that I'm probably the only person who'll ever see Shy behaving like this; if ever she spots anybody else while we are doing our lessons, she goes straight back into fright mode. I hope with time she'll get better but I doubt if she'll ever manage to perform in front of a crowd.

Janet only lives a few doors from us and as Shy and I will be passing her house this morning on our walk, we'll call in and see her; I'm interested to see how Shy will react. She's fine until Janet opens the door when she gets very frightened and almost pulls out of her collar to run away. It's hard to believe how such a simple act, the sort of thing we just take for granted can send her into such a panic. It is such a shame.

Shy is now learning to sit and wait before I let her eat her meal. We've bought her a special bowl that stops her gulping her food down; it works well and she finishes her meal after

Sheba now. At least her tummy will be able to digest the food better and soon she'll learn that nobody else is going to eat her meal so she doesn't have to rush to finish it anymore.

I am doing more work with Shy when Buffy is in the garden. She is very nervous but even more so when she sees Caroline than with Buffy, so perhaps the dogs at least, are starting to accept one another.

Shy escapes again onto the canal towpath; the problem is the hedges are so thin at this time of the year that more gaps seem to appear daily. I'm going to walk the dogs on the other side of the field away from the canal from now on and trust she will learn she shouldn't be on the other side of the hedge. At the moment it seems to be turning into a habit but it's one that needs to be stopped.

I put Shy's lead on to meet Janet and Rebecca today; up until now she's always been loose and I want to know how she'll behave when she can't run away from them. In the event, she's quite good but while we are all talking, an aggressive German Shepherd starts barking and snarling at Sheba through the hedge until the dog's owner manages to get his dog away. This really frightens Shy, which is a shame as things had been going well up until then. Once she calms down a bit, I give her the lead to carry as she loves having something in her mouth it helps to take her mind off the skirmish but when she gets into the car, I can't get it back off her, she won't give it to me, so I have to leave it with her. It's all chewed up by the time we arrive home!

It's our turn to have the children again today and Shy makes big steps by coming into the kitchen while they are in there. They seem very fond of her, spending quite a lot of time sitting by her basket and stroking her; I feel more confident that she won't snap at them now and as her confidence seems to be growing, I hope it won't be long before she starts to really enjoy their company.

Well, another four weeks have passed and we have made great strides forward but almost as many backwards. Shy is a dog that has started to feel her paws and that's just what we want; she has to make mistakes so that we are able to show her the correct way but I feel very proud of what she has achieved so far. The bond between us is growing stronger and stronger and I'm very confident the forward strides will outnumber the back strides in the weeks to come.

Shy's Hunger to Learn

Shy's ability to jump is coming on in leaps and bounds (excuse the pun.). The jumps I'm putting up for her are quite high now but nothing seems to worry her. It's rare now for her to run under the jump, she just flies over them. It's another way for her to channel her energy, have fun, and put the past behind her.

Because she's doing so well, I am going to have a go at teaching her to weave through poles. In the past, I've used plastic electric fence posts pushed into the ground to form a straight line, just leaving enough space in between for the dog to weave through. So I go in search for some posts and manage to find five, which I think will be plenty for her first attempt.

As I have done in the past when asking Shy to do something for the first time, I always ask Sheba to perform first. I can't say weaving is one of Sheba's favourite pastimes but she duly obliges. I put Shy's lead on and with a titbit in my other hand, I guide her through the posts; she's baffled at first but after several attempts, she starts to catch on. We finish on a good note when she manages to weave without her lead on; I know she is only following the titbit but it is a good start.

Two frosty mornings this week, so I take the opportunity to walk the dogs to the field. Shy is walking so much better; cars aren't too much of a problem but people still are. Luckily, we only meet a few, so for the main part we can all enjoy the walks.

Her 'stays' are coming on well and she's learning to sit and stay with Sheba when asked to do so. This is very useful because there are occasions when I need to leave the dogs if I don't want them to follow me through the very muddy patch outside the horse shelters, and I can't fault her mealtime stays, they've come on really well.

As I've said, Shy loves carrying something in her mouth, so this morning while I am leading Lady, our little old pony, I give Shy the end of Lady's lead rope. She happily follows me with Lady following her. It really amuses me; this little dog can learn anything.

Shy is getting better with Janet and Rebecca, not running so far away from them this week. Daniel pays us a visit and he thinks Shy is coming on too; he can see a big difference since the last time he saw her. She's getting closer to John, which is a good sign and I've been trying to teach her to roll over, so far, she can only manage halfway.

December

Playing ball is the one thing Shy loves most; her enthusiasm is incredible and I'm starting to think she would play until she drops if I let her. I'm now asking her to sit before I take the ball from her. She finds this difficult; all she wants is to have the ball thrown again as soon as possible, for her to chase after it. We need to keep practising.

Shy holds the lead rope for me again today, but this time it is while I am leading Zak, my very handsome Arab gelding. Zak has a brilliant temperament and is the kindest, most generous horse you could ever wish to meet, so I know he won't do anything to hurt Shy. The four of us walk towards the shelters; me in front, Shy leading Zak and Sheba bringing up the rear as all good shepherd dogs do. It feels like it's meant to be – something we have always done – an unforgettable moment.

Shy is getting more used to Caroline and Buffy; she's not quite so jumpy when they're around. In the evenings when I'm sitting down, Shy is getting very fussy over me, she cannot get enough attention. I make allowances for her because I know she's never had anyone she's been able to get close to before but tonight when Sheba comes over to see me, Shy snaps at her. I retaliate by smacking her on the nose and telling her "NO" and she quickly runs away. I feel she is trying to possess me and I must put a stop to it; Sheba is entitled to as much attention from me as Shy is.

If I don't remember to put the tea towels out of her reach when I go to bed, Shy has developed the habit of chewing off the corners. I don't know why, or what she's getting out of it, unless she thinks she can smell food on them; it can be a bit irritating but nothing to get too upset about.

I think Shy senses that I'm not feeling too well this week, because as soon as I start to feel better she appears to be in a much happier mood.

As I'm not taking the dogs to the field so much lately, we are playing ball a lot more in the garden and I'm still practicing walking Shy past Caroline and Buffy to try to boost her confidence when they are around; some days she is better than others. She still enjoys her jumping, so I make a row of jumps to follow along the side of the path running down the garden. Now, every time we go out the dogs jump the jumps while I walk down the path.

It doesn't seem quite so much of a shock now for Shy when the grandchildren come round but she still spends most of the time in her basket when they are here. However, she is starting to come out more, especially when they're eating and it always amuses us how she rushes to the front door when they're leaving, as if she's saying goodbye to them. It's more likely she's making sure they really are going; as she often lets out a deep sigh of relief before we can all settle down again to enjoy the peace and quiet.

Sibling Rivalry

This week starts well but Shy blots her copybook by snapping at Sheba again; it happens when she's having a cuddle with me and Sheba wants a bit of fuss at the same time. I think she is getting a bit jealous of Sheba. It's lucky though for Shy, that Sheba doesn't retaliate but I do. I smack her on the nose again and shout "NO" at her; she has to learn that she really must not do that.

We walk to the field four times this week. The first time, we meet a lot of traffic on the way and Shy gets very nervous. On the way back, we meet one of our neighbours and Shy just stops, frozen to the spot – she will not walk past her. So we stand and chat for a while which gives Shy a chance to weigh up the situation and relax a little. By the time we finish talking, she is relaxed enough to carry on walking home.

On our second walk Shy is a lot calmer and there is hardly any traffic, which helps a lot. She's good in the field and shows no interest in getting onto the canal towpath; I hope that habit is now well and truly broken.

Our third walk is even better. Shy is much less nervous and cars don't worry her at all. We even meet the man who lives next door to the field and Shy shows no interest in him either nothing seems to bother her today.

Our fourth walk goes well too, until we meet a cyclist, something we have not met before and it comes as no surprise when Shy tries to pull out of her collar and run away. It takes a while to settle her but after that, we are able to carry on quietly, with no further problems.

Today Shy decides she wants her basket to be put into the kitchen proper; she's spending much more time with us in the kitchen now, showing us her confidence is returning and letting us know in her own way that she wants to be closer to us. We decide that now could be the right time to let her join Sheba in her sleeping quarters and we put her basket next to Sheba's. Shy shows no hesitation in jumping in so we'll wait and see how they get on through the night.

We had a nice quiet night with no noise from the kitchen, so I presume the dogs also had a good night's sleep. It's nice to find Shy has been clean through the night, so I give both dogs plenty of fuss and then let them out into the garden. I don't think Shy's basket will need to move back to its old spot; she has well and truly moved in. Shy is becoming a real part of our family; she comes and joins us more in the lounge and I really feel she doesn't want to be left out anymore. She wants to be with us.

The Poem

A friend of ours gave us this poem when she heard that we had adopted Shy. She also has an adopted, ex-racing greyhound, which had suffered very badly. He had been owned by a very unfeeling cruel man who decided, that after the dog's racing career had ended, he would get rid of the dog himself. This he did in the worst possible way, leaving the poor creature for dead in a ditch, having first blinded him and kicked him so badly that his ribs and some of his legs were broken.

The dog wasn't quite dead and was found by some passers-by who phoned for a vet. It would have been the kindest thing for the vet to put him to sleep there and then but if there was any chance of catching and prosecuting this evil person, they had to try to keep him alive as evidence. The dog must have had a very strong will to live, because he did survive and they were able to catch and prosecute the man. But whatever punishment he received, it couldn't ever be as bad as the cruelty he inflicted upon the wretched creature; a dog that in his racing career, had undoubtedly given his best just to line the pockets of this undeserving human. He at least was entitled to a happy retirement. More and more people are finding out that ex-racing greyhounds make lovely pets, like our daughter for instance; Buffy is a lovely dog and is now enjoying her retirement with Caroline. Buffy came from a greyhound re-homing centre, so there's no excuse for anyone to abuse their dog when they're of no further use; there are lots of kind people out there who would eagerly re-home one of these very deserving graceful animals.

If it hadn't been for our friend, I doubt if this poor animal would have had much of a life left for him; she took him on and nursed him back to health, giving him all the love and attention he so badly needed. He's been her sole companion for many years now and she takes him everywhere, even though he is blind; and she never misses the chance to try to educate people on the cruelty that seems to be endemic where ex-racing greyhounds are concerned.

Whenever money is involved, it always seems to bring the worst out in some people. Like the poor puppy farm dogs for instance: if people didn't pay such high prices for puppies, there would be no puppy farms. They're only there to make as much money as possible for the keepers, with precious little going for the upkeep of the poor dogs. Are these breeders so blinded by money, they can't see that without the breeding dogs, they would have no business? Even a little kindness would help give these poor animals a better life and kindness costs nothing. So why can't they look after them better?

After reading this poem, I feel it really had to be included in my book.

BECACE OF YOU (Author Unknown)

BECAUSE OF YOU (Author Unknown)

Because of you
Tomorrow I shall see another morn
I shall hear the birds singing as they wait to greet the dawn
I shall feel the power of the sun as she gently warms me through
And I'll revel in the coolness of the early morning dew.
Because of you
I now know love and kindness I never knew before
It reached down and enfolded me as I walked through that door
So for the first time in my life
I now feel safe and sound
And thus you see before you a gentle happy hound.
Because of you
My past has gone, dispensed with, swept away
I was hungry, sore and tired and dreaded each new day
I have no happy memories
I don't like looking back
For then my only future was a large black plastic sack.

But I'm just one of thousands
A tiny grain of sand
Yet you saw the need in me
And reached out with your hand.
Because of you
Who gives so much, are generous to a 'T'
In this sad world, there's still a chance
To save a dog like me

You ask for nothing in return
And I have nowt to give
Except my wagging tail which says
Because of you – I live!

Another Milestone

Shy is still improving when she's around Janet and Rebecca, while the urge to escape from the field seems to be a thing of the past. I think she knows where the boundaries are now and she seems happy to stay within them.

Adam pops in to see us and tries to stroke Shy but she is still too frightened to let him. While he's with us, I put Shy's lead on and we sit together in the kitchen. I want to show her that no-one is going to hurt her; while we're talking I notice that Shy is starting to relax. I need to do more of this, to get her out of the habit of shooting off to her basket; I hope when she realises she is not the focus of attention, she might let go of her fears a little.

Tuesday is a good day; Shy does some excellent heelwork, even with Caroline and Buffy bobbing about. She also seems much more relaxed when she's in her basket and is also much better when John's around. Wednesday is a bit of a wipe out; I wake up with a very bad headache and am sick. John sees to the horses for me, taking Sheba with him, leaving Shy at home.

Another easy day, I still don't feel like doing too much but in the afternoon, I have to go to the field to get everything ready for the farrier who is coming tomorrow. John and the dogs come with me and the dogs seem to appreciate the outing, behaving themselves very well.

I'm feeling much better today, so after the farrier has gone, we decide to give the dogs a real treat; we'll take them to the Worcester Countryside Centre. We think Shy is ready now, something we hadn't expected for quite a few months yet, if ever; she has been such a good little girl lately and we feel that the timing is right.

With the two dogs in the car, we set off. Sheba seems to have has guessed we are not going to the field. She knows the route we take to the Countryside Centre and is starting to get very excited. Shy on the other hand, doesn't have a clue where we are going. She is getting quite stressed and because the park is a lot further than the field, it must have upset her stomach because she goes to the toilet in the car. We can't stop to clean it up, it would be too dangerous on the side of the road, so all we can do is wait until we arrive but with both dogs fidgeting around in the back, the car is getting into quite a state.

It's a great relief to drive onto the car park at the centre. We don't mess around but get out of the car as fast as possible. I go around to the back and slowly open the tailgate to reach in and get hold of Shy's collar but she is too fast for me, forcing her way through the opening and neither John nor I are quick enough to catch her. She is loose in the car park!

We shut the door to stop Sheba following which she's keen on doing but the thought of having two dogs on the loose is mind blowing. Shy is racing around us just like she does at home when she is frightened; we keep calling to her but she is too scared to come and I'm really starting to panic now. If any other cars drive in, she could easily get run over, or if she makes a bolt for it she could end up on the busy road that passes the park, where she won't stand a chance. Everything flashes through my head – we could lose her here – we shouldn't have brought her; it's too soon.

However, as luck would have it, there is no movement in the car park and Shy's circling gets smaller until she's almost within reaching distance. John opens the side door and we call to her to get in. She runs around the car a couple more times and then jumps in and we instantly shut the door behind her.

We stand for a moment gathering our wits, knowing full well how lucky we've been.

This mustn't happen again, so we make sure she can't get out until her lead is attached, then we put Sheba's lead on and get both dogs out of the car together. John holds them while I clean out the back of the car as best I can but it'll have to wait for a proper deep clean when we get home.

Now at last the walk can begin; I don't know about John but for me a stiff drink wouldn't go amiss! Shy is very jumpy and the good heelwork she's been doing at home has gone; she's all over the place, right back to the beginning of her training. But – it is her first time on a lead in a strange new place, with people, dogs, and children running around and it must be terrifying for her. We know however, that when we get on the walk proper, we'll be in large, quiet, well-fenced fields and we hope she'll settle down.

We let Sheba loose and she races off to enjoy herself. I've brought Shy's long lead so we give her the full length of it and she starts to sniff about and take in her new surroundings. She's beginning to settle a bit as we leave the children's play area behind with all its hustle and bustle. Now we're walking in lovely, large open fields with no other distractions, I hope it will remind Shy of being in her own field back home so she can relax and start to have some fun. She's certainly interested when I pick up a stick and throw it a little way for her and starts to shed her anxieties as she rushes towards it. When we're completely sure there is no-one else around, we let her lead drop and although it is dragging behind her, she's free. She goes to join Sheba and they walk together in front of us. It is a pleasure to watch and all the earlier mishaps are forgotten in an instant. This is what we have been working to achieve and the reward is in front of us with all the hard work starting to pay off. We can start to relax and enjoy the walk; the first of many, I hope. The journey home is trouble free, with two very contented dogs, and two very happy humans; long may it last!

Shy's First Christmas

Christmas is getting very close now and I'm spending a lot of time getting things ready for the big day. We've decorated the house and wonder what reaction we will get from Shy when she first sees all the tinsel and lights in the living room. She surprises us by taking no notice of them at all, being more concerned about the cracklings the fire makes every now and again. Sheba on the other hand loves a fire, settling herself on the hearthrug and soaking up the warmth. I don't doubt that Shy will try and join her before too long.

It's Christmas Eve, and Janet and Ray are coming round this evening for a pre-Christmas drink with us. Shy probably won't want to show her face, so we're not surprised when she disappears into the kitchen as they arrive. We leave it a while before I go and put her lead on and bring her into the living room, where she sits quietly beside me and as she relaxes, she begins to jump up on me as she normally does, trying to get on my lap. She doesn't seem as worried as she might be, though of course, she has met Janet before but Ray is still a stranger in her eyes. After a while, I take the lead off to see what she will do and at first, she disappears into the dining room but when her curiosity gets the better of her, she keeps coming back to peep at us through the door and eventually, she gets brave enough to come and sit with me. We have a lovely evening, made all the better by Shy's courageous behaviour

We've arranged to go to Daniel and Michelle's for Christmas dinner and normally, we would take Sheba with us but we know Shy won't be able to cope with the new surroundings and it would be unfair to take her. So after we've taken them for their morning run, John and I open our presents and happily watch as the dogs open theirs. Shy soon gets the hang of it after watching Sheba excitedly ripping off the layers of paper to find the toy or treat hidden inside; when we leave they are both contentedly lying in their baskets chewing on one of the many bones they've had as presents and we know they'll be content until we get back.

Boxing Day and Shy sees her first fox. In the past, it was the tradition to hold hunts on Boxing Day and our local hunt always used to meet at the pub opposite our field. Now though, it's as if the fox knows he is safe as he jauntily flaunts himself as he crosses our field. Sheba spots the cocky little soul and chases him, followed half-heartedly by Shy who hasn't a clue what she's after but thinks she'd better join in. The fox gets away, which is no surprise.

This morning they see the fox again and this time, Shy is keen and keeps up with Sheba as they race after it. I know they don't have a chance but I'm worried if the fox runs onto the towpath, they'll follow. It does but they don't; what a relief.

For the first time Shy goes out with John and Sheba for her nightly outing before bed. Until now, she would only go if I took her out, so to give her a better chance of going through the night without an accident, I have to stay up later than normal and as I'm not a night owl, I find this quite tiring. John on the other hand doesn't mind staying up, so it's quite a relief when Shy lets him take her out. He's stuck with that job now, thank goodness!

It depends on the weather if the dogs come with me to the field or not. It's a bit hit-and-miss but whatever the heavens throw at us, I always try to play with them for some part of the day as Shy still needs to play ball to release her energy and tension. Things are still going well when we do manage to get to the field and she's not quite so anxious when she sees Janet and Rebecca; I've also noticed she's sleeping a lot more during the day, which must be because she is learning to relax at last.

Shy's New Year

January

New Year's Eve and we are expecting fireworks; I'm not too worried about the horses; although there is a pub opposite their field, they don't usually do fireworks on New Year's Eve so there's probably no need to worry about them and I hope the dogs will be as good as they were on bonfire night. Sheba does bark a bit during the night but Shy is very good. It just goes to show that if it hadn't been for her bad experiences with humans, she would be a very well-adjusted dog. Her New Year has begun and I can see only better times ahead for Shy; the progress she has made in the short time she's been with us has been remarkable and hopefully, the improvement will continue.

It's a very cold morning and I know the ground will be hard in the field so it's a good day to take the dogs with me. I'm surprised to find that the pub did have New Year fireworks and the remains are strewn over our field. The horses have been upset and I can see they've been running around because of all the muddy hoof prints scattered about. I'm not happy about Zak, who doesn't seem to be himself, he's very quiet and I put it down to the trauma of the night; I make a note to check on him later. The dogs have a great time and the cold fresh air seems to give them a new lease of life but I'm worried about Zak and the walk isn't so much fun for me.

PART FOUR

Heartache

The Loss of a Beloved Friend

If I could erase the next few weeks from my life, I would; they have been the most worrying and saddest times I can recall.

I'm not sure why I don't take the dogs to the field with me today, the weather isn't too bad so they could have come but I decide to leave them at home with John. It's our turn to have the children and I don't want to be too long; it'll be quicker without the dogs.

I see that Zak is standing on his own in the field and not with his friends, which is not like him; he's always first in the queue to get his treats. I attend to the other horses and then go across to him. "What's the matter boy?" I say as I approach him. He half-heartedly tries to eat his treats but makes no attempt to move which is very worrying and when I ask him to walk with me to the shelters, he won't budge. I phone John and fight back the tears as I tell him about Zak. He says he will come straight down but he'll have to bring the children with him.

By now, Janet and Rebecca have arrived and can see there is a problem; Rebecca crosses the field to join us and with her walking behind Zak and me in front, we manage to get him to the shelters; he is completely lame. I realise we'll have to walk him up the lane to get him home but I'm not sure he'll make it.

By the time John arrives, Rebecca and I have managed to get Zak to the shelters but he looks very poorly; we decide that John will try to lead Zak while Rebecca and Janet walk behind to encourage him to move forward. The children will come with me in the car, so I can get home to prepare his stable and to phone the vet.

As I drive past the little group, walking so very slowly up the lane, Zak is bravely doing his best to manage what must seem like the longest walk he's ever had to make. I feel tears start to run down my face. My poor horse, will he make it? What on earth will we do if he can't? I doubt if he'll have the strength to return to the field and might even collapse in the road. With these thoughts running through my mind, I get home as fast as I can, put the children in the house and ask them to play nicely while I go and sort Zak's stable out for him.

It's such a relief when I see them arrive. As we put Zak in his stable, his ears come up and he seems as relieved as we are to be home and Janet remarks on how much happier he looks. All we have to do now is to wait for the vet to arrive.

I know our vet won't mess us about. If he thinks Zak needs to be put down he will say so but I'm dreading what he might say. When he arrives, I can tell from his face that it's serious but he gives Zak a thorough going over and says he thinks it isn't time for him to go just yet. He gives him a couple of injections and tells us not to keep him shut in the stable but to let him come and go as he pleases, with a warning that if he lies down, he might not be able to get back up and then we will have a problem. After about an hour the injections start to kick in and Zak seems to be more comfortable; he manages to potter out and have a little nibble at some grass; things start to look a bit better and I can start to breathe again. The dogs have to take a back seat and the children have to amuse themselves, as John and I spend most of the rest of the day popping in and out attending to Zak.

Zak makes it through the night and things do start to look brighter; he appears to be a bit stronger and I guess the injections are still working. I'm not able to give much attention to the dogs and all my time is taken up with Zak. We have a fright in the afternoon when he lies down and after what the vet has said this is very scary. We leave him for a bit but it starts to rain and we don't know what to do; he looks awful just lying flat out in the rain. We stand it for a while but then decide to try to get him up; John puts his head collar and lead rope on and asks him to get up and he tries but can't manage it at first. Then he makes a real effort and scrambles to his feet and we slowly get him back to the stable and out of the rain.

Zak is very lame again this morning and I think the effort of standing has made his leg worse and the injections are now wearing off. I phone the vet and ask if he'll come to see him again. When he arrives, he looks relieved and comments how much better the horse looks in himself since the last time he saw him. I think he'd been expecting the worst. He gives Zak some more injections and tells us to carry on with what we had been doing. "There's no quick fix," he says; "it could take months." We don't mind; we'll do anything we can to help Zak get well again.

If it's true that dogs can sense your moods, I think Shy has picked up on mine; she jumps up and gives me hugs – and I mean hugs – her little legs so tightly wrapped around my waist that I can barely move. She is doing her best to cheer me up and it's working.

In the following week, my time is mostly taken up with looking after Zak. The dogs are being very good and do not put me under any pressure to take them to the field. They seem to understand and stay very close to me, lying down quietly while I am attending to Zak and watching with great interest as I massage his legs and give him healing. I couldn't wish for a better-behaved audience and I know Zak enjoys having them around; its company for him.

We do manage to get there on a couple of mornings though. The first time is a big mistake as the ground is very muddy and the dogs come back hardly recognizable. The second morning is much better as it's very frosty and the ground is nice and hard. Shy seems in a very happy mood and after jumping out of the car, she comes across to me and does the whole huggy thing again. We have a very relaxing walk, giving me some time to chill out and let go of the worry over Zak if only for a short while; I am in real need of it.

The next week is much the same except Shy has a setback in the toilet department and we have a few accidents in the kitchen. She's quite edgy lately; her routine has changed and she must be picking up on the tense atmosphere. Although I try to keep things as normal as possible it's hard, as I am still very worried about Zak. I can't be cross with her, it's not her fault; it's just the situation we are in.

Saturday is not a good day. Zak lies down in his stable and can't get up. It's awful; he tries so hard but he just can't make it. Just as I'm about to call the vet, Daniel arrives, and with his help, we manage to get Zak to his feet. I really thought we were going to have to have him put down, it was a very close call, but for the moment at least we still have him. After Daniel leaves, John and I return to the house, both feeling like all our life's energy has been drained from us. If it hadn't been for Daniel, we would have lost Zak today and we know we might not be so lucky if it happens again; our poor Zak is teetering on the edge. It's not surprising the dogs are finding life hard right now – they must sense the draining of our energy and the sadness we are both feeling.

The weather is awful; rain, rain and more rain. There seems to be no let up and it matches my mood in every way. I feel so depressed. Even if Zak wasn't at home, I wouldn't be taking the dogs down to the field. I've noticed though, that they're playing much more with each other recently. I think it's because they are spending a lot more time in the garden, and releasing their energy by having little rough and tumbles with each other. It's lovely to watch, there's no nastiness between them, they're just playing.

Shy is learning to shake a paw. When Sheba gives me her paw, it's very gentle but when Shy does it, it's more like a slap. I must trim her claws, especially the dew claws which are very sharp, if they catch my hand when she gives me a slap I end up with a nasty scratch.

I always try and make time to play with the dogs, even if we don't manage to get to the field. We dodge in and out between the never-ending showers. Shy really lets off steam, tearing round and round the garden. She doesn't often behave like this but it's always fun to watch. I guess it's because she's not getting enough exercise to use her energy up. I really hope the weather will change soon; I think the dogs too, are starting to feel fed up.

John is approaching his 75th birthday and all the family are coming to help him celebrate. I've been busy cleaning the house and baking various things for his special day and I hope it won't be too much for Shy to handle; there will be quite a houseful, more people than she's ever seen since she's been living with us.

Although it's John's birthday today, Shy seems to be the star attraction. Everybody wants to see her, so one by one they all troop into the kitchen to take a look while she does her usual thing, lying in her basket quietly taking it all in. Everybody thinks she's lovely and the grandchildren are adamant that they want a dog and it must be like Shy. I do not think Sheba's feelings are hurt, she knows she is the number one really.

Shy is shaking her paw really well now and I'm not getting so scratched since I clipped her claws. She is going more to John but she still has good and bad days and it's not helping that she is not getting enough exercise to release her tensions. We still play ball a lot but it's not the same as going to the field. I think we must be having the wettest January on record; it certainly seems like it

February

Shy is still improving when the grandchildren come to visit. It would be lovely if one day we'll see her running around and playing with them. They still think the world of Shy and the days are gone when Ellie hardly ever spoke; there are even times now when John and I laughingly say "bring back the good old days let's have a bit of hush."

I'm still spending a lot of time popping in and out to see to Zak and the children are being very good and behaving themselves most of the time. I haven't been able to give them as much attention as I would like but John is being great and seeing to all their needs.

I'm really impressed with Shy's heelwork today. It's about four weeks since she had her last lesson but she remembers everything she's been taught. I think I enjoy the lesson as much as she does and it makes a lovely change.

It's Monday, the start of a new week – and guess what – it's stopped raining. So the dogs and I can go to the field. It's still very muddy but the dogs have a great time so it's well worth the mess they're in when we arrive home.

Back to rain again. We are all getting so fed up that it comes as no surprise when Sheba makes a few little snaps at Shy, purely out of boredom. I've just got to take them into the garden whether it's raining or not. I know they are always with me when I am seeing to Zak but they need to be able to let off steam and the only way they can do this is by chasing the ball. Luckily they still find this fun but it's not so much fun for me when I'm trying to dry them both off before going back inside. The whole house has an unpleasant smell of wet dogs and my wellingtons and wet coat don't help the situation.

The weather does not improve for the rest of the week but luckily, Zak is able to come and go in his stable and appears to be getting stronger so that we're beginning to feel more optimistic about his future. I couldn't wish for a better patient; he is such a good lad.

The farrier is due and as Zak's feet need trimming, I've asked him to come to the house to do Zak after he's done the others. Looking back, I think this was a mistake. Zak seemed to be getting better but he was obviously not as well as I thought. This morning, after the farrier, he is very lame again, as lame as when we first brought him home; it's been too much for him. I increase his painkillers and decide to phone Christine, a friend of ours who is a horse chiropractor and healer, to come and see if she can help him. I've often used her in the past and have always been impressed with the treatment she has given to my horses.

Christine arrives and is very upset at how she finds Zak. She's treated him many times and always comments on what a lovely horse he is. He's a very special animal almost human, she says, and I agree. We get Zak into his stable and she lets her hands run over him to find out where the pain is coming from. I don't say anything; I want to see if she feels the pain in the same place as I did. At first, she is puzzled; "I can't seem to find anything," she says and then lets out a gasp; she has found the spot, right at the top of his hind leg. I nod; "yes that's where it is." The pain is very deep and Christine wonders if he has cracked a bone. Oh, I do hope not; I know the outcome will be bleak if he has.

She gives him a thorough going over, putting back parts of his body into place that are out of line and then finishes with a very intense healing session. Zak looks very relaxed when Christine leaves and the pain I've been seeing on his face has disappeared; he looks at ease for the first time in weeks.

I slept well tonight, better than I've done for a while – Zak is at peace and so am I. He's looking much better this morning, walking around and showing more interest in things, even shooing the dogs off when they get too close to his food and calling to me when he wants my attention. I give him a big hug, feeling he really is on the mend.

Christine visited Zak on Tuesday and on Saturday; she phones to see how he's getting on. She is so pleased to hear how well things are going and I feel happier than I have in weeks; a weight has been lifted off my shoulders and it feels great.

But on Sunday morning when I go to prepare Zak's breakfast, I am surprised to find he is lying down in his stable. It doesn't worry me too much at first as I think he is strong enough now to manage to get to his feet; I mix his breakfast and take it into him. He wants his feed and tries very hard to get up but he just can't do it, his spirit is willing but his body isn't. My heart sinks; I rush back into the house to tell John the bad news and he comes back out with me to see him.

Of all the places Zak could lie down, he had to go and pick the stable; it's not helping him to get up; his feet can't get any grip, they just keep sliding and the more he tries, the more exhausted he gets. He would stand a better chance if we can get him outside, but how on earth do we do that?

Gripping at straws, I phone Daniel. He helped get Zak up before and maybe he can do it again. It's very hard to speak to him, the lump in my throat keeps getting in the way. He can tell how upset I am and says he will be over shortly, telling me to keep him calm and not to let him try to get up, saving all his energy until he comes. Daniel is full of common sense and I always put a lot of trust in him.

He arrives, bringing our other two sons with him. I am so relieved to see them all, if they can't get Zak on his feet, no-one can. We all try hard but the main effort has to come from Zak and he just can't push with his back legs. The only way he has any chance at all is to get him outside where the ground is softer and his legs might have something to push against, giving him more grip to help him stand.

How they did it I will never know but they managed it and Zak looks much happier now he is outside. We prop him up with some bales of hay and he lies there quite happily, munching a big bowl of feed and nibbling at the hay. We hope when he's had a rest he might regain some strength and manage to get up. During the afternoon, he makes several attempts but he still can't make it so with night approaching, we realise he'll have to spend the night outside. The only piece of luck we have is the weather, which after days of non-stop rain is now dry; in fact it's a lovely evening, very mild and pleasant. We go to bed knowing that if Zak doesn't manage to get up in the night, we will have to have him put down in the morning.

In the middle of the night, I get out of bed and walk down the garden with a torch to check Zak. He's still lying down and I'm amused to hear him snoring softly; he's not unduly worried then. He looks surprised when he opens his eyes and sees me standing there and I push the hay bales more under him as they have moved; I guess when he was trying to get up. I cover him back over with his sheet and give him some peppermints, his most favourite treat, and then leave him in peace. I know in my heart this will be the last night he will spend with us, he has suffered enough, and it is time to let go.

Zak is still lying down this morning, so with a very heavy heart I go back into the house and phone the vet on a special number because it's out of hours and the surgery isn't open yet. The person on the other end tells me they will contact the vet and she will phone me back. The call comes quickly and I explain what the situation is and that I'm expecting the worst. She says she will be with me in about twenty minutes. I spent the time sitting by Zak, stroking and talking to him, saying my goodbyes. I cut a piece of his beautiful tail to keep forever.

It seems like no time at all before the vet arrives. Seeing her, Zak makes one last effort to rise and then lies back down. She looks on, knowing there is no hope and that the kindest thing will be to put him down. I couldn't have wished for a kinder person to be with me in the last moments of Zak's life; she said all the right things.

I tell her how we'd got him out of the stable, hoping it would help him get to his feet. I said I don't think we should have done that but she said we'd given him every chance and that nature can be a marvellous thing; it might have worked and we shouldn't beat ourselves up for trying.

When I tell her we've had him since he was a foal, she's surprised. It's unusual for her to come across a horse of twenty-two, who has had the same owner all his life. Horses usually have many owners and she said Zak had been a very lucky boy. She thinks he's probably got a broken leg and because it's a hind leg, nothing can be done. She asks if I want to stay while she gives Zak his injection.

"Yes" I say; "I want to be with him to the end." And she seems pleased about this as owners often can't bear to watch but on many occasions I've had it said to me 'doesn't your horse look after you' and he always did; so I'm not going to leave him in his final moments.

Zak drifts off to sleep free of pain forever and my beloved horse lies there, at peace. The vet makes all the arrangements for Zak to be collected and taken away for cremation and I'm very grateful; I don't think I can cope with much more. After the vet has gone, we cover Zak over, and go and have a cup of tea while we wait for the man to arrive.

We don't have to wait very long, he is with us within the hour, and I leave John to see to the rest. I've said farewell and I don't want to watch Zak's body being loaded into the trailer. The man asks what name we want to be on the casket of Zak's ashes and we go for his posh name of Kabisa, with Zak in brackets. Then they're gone. My boy has gone forever. Writing this has been hard for me. Even after all these months, it is still very raw for me and the tears are still flowing.

Life Goes on

John and I need something to take our minds off the day's happenings and since it's still early, we load the dogs into the car and head off to the Countryside Centre, where hopefully, we can relax a bit and come to terms with what has happened. The journey goes well, no messes in the car from Shy, and getting her out of the car goes without a hitch. It's a good job, because neither of us are in the right frame of mind to cope with her escaping again.

The walk around the park is just what we needed; Shy is much more relaxed than on her first visit and that in turn, rubs off on us. We're in no hurry to go home, we stroll around just breathing in the lovely fresh air, letting our minds and bodies repair themselves after the trauma of the past few weeks. I don't think any of us wants the walk to end and I can hardly bear the thought of going back to find an empty stable, knowing I will never see Zak again.

John and I are very down this morning and the dogs pick up on the atmosphere but all credit to them, they are both behaving very well. I notice I'm getting a lot more hugs from Shy and I think she's feeling my sadness. At least the weather has improved and I can take the dogs to the field where they can let off steam and I can quietly walk behind them and try to get to grips with my feelings.

The other horses must be wondering where their mate is. It might have been better if they'd seen Zak when he died so they could have accepted the fact but as it is, it'll quite some time before they realise he isn't coming back. I am sure they can sense how sad I am and maybe they understand; I'd like to think they do.

Whenever sad times come into my life, the only way I seem to be able to cope is by throwing myself into a project to try to take my mind off things. During the time of Zak's illness, I started to paint a picture of Sheba and Shy lying down in the grass together. It may not be the best picture I've ever painted but it helped me a great deal at the time.

It's Friday and we decide to take the dogs to our local park, another first for Shy, and another chance for John and I to turn our thoughts to something different. Shy's very nervous and doesn't want to pass any other dogs or people, so John has to lead the way with Sheba. There's a part of the park away from the children's play area where dogs can be loose, so when the coast is clear we let the dogs off their leads and Shy starts to relax. She's not straying too far from us and we can see she's beginning to enjoy the walk. When it's over, we put the dogs back in the car and head for home, pleased with how Shy behaved on another first in her life.

The Dream

March

In the following weeks, I have a mixture of emotions. Some days I am able to come to terms with what has happened but on others, I hit rock bottom. I keep wondering if I could have done things differently and start to blame myself for Zak's death – if only I'd noticed his problems sooner when he was under the weather after those wretched fireworks! Maybe if I'd brought him home that day and not waited until he could hardly walk – or delayed having the blacksmith – the list goes on and on. I feel that I let him down when he needed me most and at times it feels like I'm losing my mind. The dogs help to get me through the days but the worst time is when I am sitting quietly on my own. I can't get Zak out of my thoughts. I am grieving and anyone who's been through it, whether for an animal or human, will know what I mean. John can't help me as he's going through his own grief; we just can't help each other.

I can't get the picture out of my head of the first time I met Zak. I'd been toying with the idea of putting my old mare Donna, an Arab x Cob into foal but she was getting on a bit and I decided against it. Knowing this, a friend of mind told me about an Arab foal coming up for sale shortly so I phoned the number she gave me and spoke to the woman selling the foal. She sounded very nice but was almost apologetic about Zak's colouring. She said he was a nondescript colour at the moment but that he would eventually turn into a grey. I didn't really know what to expect but we arranged to go over and meet him. To say I was excited would be an understatement; I'd always wanted to own a young horse and you couldn't get much younger than a foal, it would be quite an experience.

The woman took us to the paddock where the foal and his mother were with another mare and foal, a chestnut filly, very typical flashy Arab, prancing around and making sure she got all the attention. She was lovely but my eyes were on Zak who just stood looking at us, weighing up the situation. He wasn't as brave as the filly but there was something about him; yes, he was an unusual colour – a sort of pink – but looking beyond that, I felt he was the one for me. I told the woman I liked him and John agreed. I think she was surprised, he blended into the background next to the filly but he looked as if he would be a sensible animal and I would rather have that, especially as it would be my first youngster. We agreed on a price and arranged to visit him regularly until he was old enough to leave his mother.

It took several visits before Zak was brave enough to come and meet us but I will never forget the first time he did. I was kneeling on the ground calling and holding my hand out to him as I usually did. He started to come and I held my breath, fully expecting him to dash away at the last minute but instead; he got close enough to sniff me and he must have liked what he smelt because that day we bonded and he couldn't get enough of me. I laughed and said to John; "Today we've fallen in love with each other." John was busy getting the moment on film and we've watched it many times since. The time we spent with Zak that day was very special.

I think Zak looked forward to our visits from then on; he wasn't frightened of us anymore and even started to develop a sense of humour. He would take great delight in pulling John's cap off his head and carrying it around in his mouth before depositing it on the ground; he was a cheeky little chap.

As a foal, as a yearling and as a mature horse, Zak never disappointed me. He turned out to be all I had hoped and much more. My little ugly duckling turned into a very handsome swan, a beautiful grey horse with superb manners; a perfect gentleman you might say. It's not surprising that losing him has been so hard to bear; he was a horse in a million. One day I hope I'll be able to look back and enjoy the memories but for the moment, it hurts too much.

Health-wise I don't think I am doing very well. I have begun to lose weight and I feel like all my energy has left me. It's getting harder and harder to walk the dogs and I feel exhausted most of the time but being the special pair they are, they always seem to know how to cheer me up. Things are changing; I now need Shy more than she needs me and Sheba has always been my best friend.

After losing Zak I dream of him often but there is one dream I'll never forget. I'm talking to Zak, telling him how sorry I am and how much I love him. Zak turns to me and says in a very clear voice; "I love you too; please don't worry about me, I'm fine but you really must look after yourself." I wake with a jolt – it's as clear as if he were in the room with me. Someone, whether it really was Zak or not, had spoken to me; I'm sure of that. As I lie there with my heart beating fast, I reflect on the dream. He's right I think, I really do need to look after myself. I can't alter what's happened and I must stop looking back. I feel like I've been pulled back from the brink; even in a dream, Zak looks after me as he always did in life.

Life gets a bit easier after that and I'm able to go forward again. I have much to be happy about; I have a great husband, a lovely family, and some of the best animals I could wish for. The dogs pick up on my new mood and it shows in the way they play with each other; they're having fun again and that in turn, makes me feel good.

Even the horses seem happier and Oliver, my other Arabian horse, a handsome, strong-minded little chap, who has always been awkward and never made things easy for me [the exact opposite to Zak], seems to be more settled and is showing more patience towards me. Whether he feels he's gone up in the ranks now that Zak isn't around I don't know – but whatever it is I like it – long may it last.

Springtime

We're well into March now and the weather is slowly but surely getting better, the field is starting to dry up so the dogs are able to enjoy their walks again. Spring is always my favourite time of the year and after the last few months I think we all need something good to look forward to. Just to have days when the sun is shining and the sky is blue is a tonic in itself. We do still get rainy days of course but they are getting fewer and the dogs are feeling happier. They must have found the winter hard going with the long boring days but now at last, they can look forward to fun.

Shy is getting braver and starting to bark if someone comes to the door which always makes us laugh, because she backs away as she barks; she's going through the motions but isn't quite brave enough yet to back it up.

Shy jumps up John for the first time, which is lovely to see, but she doesn't seem very relaxed about doing it. Perhaps she thinks he's going to grab her; he still has a long way to go to get her trust but its coming.

For a change, we take the dogs for a walk into Trench Woods, which is just a stone's throw away from the field. It's a real joy watching them running in and out of the trees, tracking all the different scents. For a brief moment, Shy is putting all her fears to one side as she joins in the fun with Sheba and the fact that we do not meet anybody else while we are there helps her relax and enjoy herself more. Life would be so good for her if there were no other people on the planet.

Caroline says she and Buffy would like to come with us to the field this morning; I'm interested to see how Shy and Buffy get on with each other and actually, they're very good. Maybe Buffy doesn't think of the field as her territory and isn't so possessive over it. They've been getting on much better lately and it's lovely to see all three dogs enjoying letting off steam without any hint of an argument between them.

Sheba has an annoying habit of dropping her ball into the stream when she's having a paddle but she can't always find it again, as it gets lost in the foliage growing in the water. Today is one of those days and no matter how hard she looks, she can't find it. We have to leave it and hope we'll find it tomorrow. Of course, this leaves us with only one ball – Shy's. As Sheba is in one of her mischievous moods, she won't allow Shy to get to the ball when I throw it for her; Shy is fast but when Sheba is determined, she doesn't stand a chance. This spoils the walk as Shy really loves chasing her ball so in the end I put the ball into my pocket and the game comes to an abrupt end.

John comes with us this morning; I found another ball for Sheba to play with and things go much better. John plays ball with Shy, another first; she's getting much closer to him now. Sheba and I go in search of her lost ball and I'm pleased when we are lucky enough to find it as it's her favourite. She looks very happy trotting back to the others, proudly sporting her ball.

I don't know if it was because Shy and Sheba squabbled over the ball the other day, but Shy is getting reluctant to give me her ball; normally she's very good but she must be worrying that Sheba will take it off her; I hope this latest hang-up doesn't last very long.

Although the conditions in the field are better, it only takes a bit rain to churn it up again. We've had such a wet winter that the ground is waterlogged and any excess water can only sit on top of the ground with nowhere to go. There are still days when it rains, for several hours, so it's still hit and miss as to what state the dogs are in when they arrive home. If I'm lucky they'll have a paddle in the stream which helps a bit as it washes a lot of the mud off but by the time we walk back across the field, they're as bad as ever. Country life eh!

Shy has developed another little hang-up; she's getting awkward about jumping into the car when we're about to leave the field so I've begun to throw a treat in for her first, which seems to be working.

Overall, March has been a good month. Shy is still doing well with her lessons; her sit stays are good, her weaving is coming on well and of course, she loves her jumping. There's still a lot of work to do and when the weather really settles, we'll be able to do a lot more. But for the moment I couldn't be happier with how she is coming along.

April

At last a break in the weather; it's more settled and I feel we can go forward now. I think Shy is ready to do more obedience work, so that's our mission for April. Making the most of the nice weather, I'm trying to clear the weeds from much-neglected borders in the garden, when Daniel calls round. On seeing the dogs, he calls Shy to him. She goes quite close but then barks several times and runs round and round him; I really think she is getting braver so that can only be good.

One of the things Shy isn't keen on doing is lying down to order; she seems to feel vulnerable when she's in that position, so I've started teaching her a more relaxed 'down', where she's lying more on her side than crouching on all fours and it seems to be working.

John gets his first hug from Shy this month and it really cheers him up. To top it all, when we are in the middle of our lessons in the garden Shy spots John and runs full pelt up to him. What a difference! A few weeks ago, she would have run the other way.

We're bringing the ponies back home for a little 'holiday' as I call it. They enjoy the change and do a great job of mowing the lawn. John hardly has to mow the lawn when they're at home and that always makes him very happy! Shy seems to really enjoy being around them and shows no fear at all. She's still getting better with Janet and Rebecca, they haven't tried to stroke her yet but the fact that she isn't running so far away from them is a good sign.

Shy's going in the stream a lot more, learning that it's fun and she enjoys splashing around with Sheba. She's lying down a lot more at home now, relaxing more and enjoying life; John has his second hug.

We take the dogs on a long walk today. Shy is much more relaxed now when she's walking with us so we all have a lovely walk across fields and along the canal towpath, finishing back at our field where we let the dogs loose to let off steam and chill out. A good time is had by all.

Our little dog is turning the corner; she's beginning to enjoy simple things like rolling in the ponies' shavings and then dashing around madly for no obvious reason. A twinkle is appearing in her eyes and she's developing a sense of humour. I really think she's starting to enjoy being alive.

PART FIVE

Moving On

The Will to Survive

The two ponies Lady and Frisbee, are back in the field now, their 'holiday' is over. Today however, while I'm doing my daily check on them, I am surprised to see that Lady is lying down which is unusual for her; while I am doing my chores, I keep a watchful eye on her and notice she gets up and then lies down again several times. My heart sinks as this can only mean one thing; she has colic which can be very serious in horses and I know there's no time to lose; I phone John and he comes straight over. She's standing when he arrives so we put her head collar on to try and lead her home but we haven't gone far when she stops dead and lies down by the side of the road. Not knowing if we'll be able to get her to her feet again, we're starting to panic but after a few minutes rest the pain must have eased and she manages to stand. We turn round and take her back to the field quickly; John takes the dog's home and phones the vet.

I stay with Lady and try to comfort her. The vet arrives quite quickly but poor Lady is lying down again and I'm not sure what he'll say. She's a very old pony so he might think it's kinder to put her to sleep but after he examines her he thinks it's worth giving her a chance, as she has quite a strong heart and he can see she's a little fighter. He gives her an injection to ease the pain and then waits to see if it works. "It usually takes about fifteen minutes," he says and sure enough it does; he looks pleased and tells us to watch her and see how things go but to call him back out if she starts to get worse.

After he's gone, I look at John and say; "I think we should have another go at getting her home, we'll be able to keep a much better eye on her there". Reluctantly he agrees. I know the relief she's getting from the injection will wear off soon so we have to get a move on. Lady walks quite well up the lane but we both breathe a big sigh of relief when we reach our gate. We put her straight into Zak's old stable which still has all the shavings down from when he was last there; the painkiller starts to wear off and it's not long before she starts to get uncomfortable again, we've been lucky to make it back just in time and we spend the rest of the day checking on her. She has moments when she appears to be feeling better but she's still lying down a lot, which is not a good sign.

As I look at Lady lying there, all the memories of Zak's last moments come flooding back. I know she's old and I must prepare myself for the possibility of losing her but it's too soon; I'm still grieving; I keep saying to myself please don't let it happen again, please. I spend a lot of time talking to her, stroking her, and giving her healing. But when we go to bed, she's still no better, so I tell John that if she's still the same in the morning, I'm going to have her put to sleep; I'm not prepared to let her suffer anymore. He agrees but we have another restless night and my mind is all over the place.

Although we haven't had Lady for the whole of her life, she's been with us for many years; we got her when her owner was unable to sell her because of breathing problems and bouts of laminitis, so she reluctantly decided to have her put down. This would have been a great shame because she was a lovely little girl, full of character and very strong-minded. We had a young granddaughter at the time, who was just starting to show an interest in horses, so we decided to take Lady on and our granddaughter Cerise has had many happy times learning to ride on her.

Morning comes and I go down to the stable to check on Lady once more. I peer over the door and my heart sinks – Lady is lying down again. She is very restless and obviously in a lot of pain. She stands for a few minutes and then lies down again and I feel the tears well up in my eyes. It isn't safe for me to go into the stable because she's all over the place, so while I'm standing, looking over the half stable door, I point my hand towards her and send her the strongest healing I can muster. After a while, she settles a bit and lies down and at this point,

I think it's safe to go into her stable. I stand over her, put my hand on her stomach and I can feel the pain; it's coming and going like contractions in labour. From this, I know Lady has compacted colic, which means unless she is able to pass something soon, she will die. As I give her healing, I can hear gurgling noises start to come from her tummy-this is a good sign, it means things might be starting to happen.

"Come on Lady," I say to her "you can do it." And sure enough, after several minutes she passes what I can only describe as a small rugby ball. The relief, for both of us is mind blowing; I feel as if I'd won the lottery. Lady gets to her feet almost immediately, I open the stable door and she wanders out and starts grazing as if nothing had ever happened. I rush back into the house to tell John the good news, "Lady will live another day".

There's a spring in my step when I take the dogs to the field this morning. Lady is still doing well and is back to her old cheeky self, demanding her breakfast and looking completely unaffected by yesterday's episode. I feel great and so do the dogs but it's short-lived because when I am checking the horses, I notice now that Rosa isn't looking well. Rosa is John's horse a lovely part thoroughbred who unfortunately suffers from arthritis so she's not ridden anymore. This morning she looks stiffer than usual and isn't quite herself. I can't put my finger on it but I know I'll need to keep a careful eye on her. As I walk the dogs around the field my happy mood darkens How much more can I take? Surely, it must end soon.

I check on Rosa several times today and give her a few healing sessions. She doesn't appear to be any worse at the end of the day so John and I decide to leave her where she is for now. I'm very apprehensive when we reach the field this morning, not knowing what awaits me. I hope Rosa is better but knowing our recent track record, I am braced for the worst. To my great relief, she does seem to be a lot better. I have no idea what had made her feel bad yesterday but fingers crossed, she's on the mend. I give her some more healing, plenty of treats and loads of hugs, and leave her looking very content and relaxed.

While Rosa was having her healing, both dogs were lying at my feet quietly watching every movement, something they always do when I give healing. So because I was so cheered by Rosa's progress, I gave them some healing too, followed by a lovely relaxed walk across the field, making a fitting end to what turned out to be a super morning.

Our neighbours have two dogs; one is a Jack Russell with a big chip on his shoulder who is forever going for my two dogs through the hedge. Luckily, Sheba ignores him most of the time but occasionally she snaps back, especially if he manages to push his way through to our side. Shy usually gives him a wide birth but this morning she goes right back at him. I'm quite surprised but very pleased to see that our timid little dog is coming out of her shell.

Shy still has moments when she won't give me the ball to throw for her. It seems to hark back to when Sheba pinched her ball after she'd lost hers in the stream. No amount of coaxing does the trick and this is one of those days. Yesterday she was fine but for whatever reason, she will not give me her ball today – she just carries it around in her mouth. Knowing how she really enjoys the fun of chasing after the ball, I feel very sorry for her when we are on our walk; it's like she is missing out. So when it's time for us to go home I put Sheba in the car to see if Shy will give me the ball when there's just the two of us. At first she is very reluctant. Perhaps she thinks I'm trying to trick her into getting the ball and taking it away from her. Finally, she gives it to me and I immediately throw it for her to fetch. She chases happily after it and after that I have no more problems getting it off her. She quickly realises that Sheba can't come and spoil the game and we play for quite some time before she happily jumps back into the car puffing loudly but free of stress. I won't bring the balls with us tomorrow morning; maybe it'll give the dogs time to forget their differences.

Back home when no balls are involved, Shy and Sheba are really playing well together now, rolling around and chasing each other. Shy has moments when she wants to keep the game going; she loves having a little rough and tumble with her big sister. It's great to watch; I can see such a difference in her; she is behaving more like a normal dog.

I don't know if it's because I didn't bring the balls with me today and Shy hasn't been able to use up her energy, but she will not get back into the car when it's time to leave the field; she just won't get in. Maybe she feels cheated, we haven't played her beloved game, and as I've already discovered when Shy sets her mind, there's no way I can change it. In the end, I have to give in and lift her into the car and how I manage it, I don't know; she is surprisingly heavy. I hope this is not the start of another of her little hang-ups.

There are no problems getting Shy in the car to go to the field this morning but I take the balls this time just in case she plays up again. At least if there's a problem, I could tempt her by throwing the ball into the car first, hoping she'll jump in after it; that's the plan anyway. Shy's plan is different. She's adamant that she's not going to get into the car when home time comes. She can be so stubborn and now the ball game hasn't worked, I'm at a loss at what to do. I'll just have to play the waiting game; I certainly don't want to get into a routine of lifting her in. So I sit down on the tail gate and wait. Sheba is very patient and the main thing I've also learnt since having Shy, is patience. Sheba and I sit patiently together and Shy runs round and round the car, slowing down a bit as she passes the open door, making it look as though she's about to jump in – but then she changes her mind and carries on running. I don't know how long we sit there – a while certainly – but it's worth it in the end. She must have thought the game was getting boring so after countless laps, she jumps in. Sheba and I look at each other, both thinking the same. Thank goodness for that, let's go home.

May

Sunday May 4th and there is going to be a dog show not far from where we live. We've often said that we would take the dogs to a show when we think the time is right and this show seems to tick all the boxes. It's not going to be a huge show, it's not too far to travel and it sounds perfect to introduce Shy to another side of the doggie world. We always enjoy going to small, friendly dog shows; it's nice to mix with people who have the same interest. They are far more tolerant around dogs and, at a small show the atmosphere should be nice and light-hearted, with everybody there just to have fun. I know Shy will find it difficult at first, but hopefully when she relaxes, she'll settle and enjoy the new experience. We don't intend to enter either of the dogs in any classes, we just want to walk around and let Shy get used to the hustle and bustle of the show. And of course, there will be lots of other dogs and all dogs have owners – Shy's dreaded nightmare! I'm hoping that when she realises no one is going to grab her, she'll settle and start to enjoy herself; I'll keep my fingers crossed anyway.

The three days before the show go well. I'm now putting Shy in the car first, before Sheba and it's working because she's jumping in with no fuss but knowing Shy, it won't be long before she thinks of something else for me to work on. She seems to have much more energy recently, so I've increased the obedience lessons to try to channel it into working fun rather than boisterous activities. She does seem to love learning new things, so it feels like the right approach.

I'm making her a vest to wear at the show, explaining why she's so nervous. I'm going to write 'PEOPLE FRIGHTEN ME' on one side of it and on the other, 'RESCUED FROM PUPPY FARM ABUSE.' She's likely to get a lot of attention because of her nervousness and I think it's a good idea to explain why this is. If nothing else, it might make people more aware of how cruel these places can be and if it helps to bring an end to the awful practices, then maybe some good will have come out of Shy's misery.

Showtime

The day has arrived and John and I are full of nervous anxiety. It's the uncertainty that worries us – we want everything to go well of course but we know it will be a massive day in Shy's life. Hopefully there will be something good to remember about it for her, so that in future we'll be able to take her to another show, knowing that she'll cope and perhaps even enjoy the experience. The journey goes well. As I said, it isn't far so Shy's tummy doesn't get upset. We never have to worry about Sheba as she always travels well, even if she gets a bit excited when she realises we're going further than the field.

We arrive at the showground, and there's a nice big field set aside for cars to park on which is great, we can give the dogs a walk before we go into the show itself. We make sure Shy doesn't do her escape act again and unload the dogs quite calmly. Shy is a bit taken aback when she sees all the people and dogs milling around and is more than happy to stick as close to us as she can. We have our walk and when the dogs are settled, we head for the show. I try to appear confident, knowing animals pick up on your feelings but it's not easy. We follow John and Sheba, which helps a lot because Shy is finding it very difficult. She hates people being behind and at the side of us, but when we get away from the entrance, the crowds start to thin out and she begins to relax. I notice people are reading the message on her vest and I can hear them saying, "oh what a shame" and even asking if we know what kind of things have happened to her. Some people stop and try to stroke and talk to her but it's too soon for Shy and I can see the sadness in their eyes. Many people don't realise the cruelty that goes on in some puppy farms, so I hope our message is doing some good.

Sheba gets a lot of attention. It's quite surprising how popular German Shepherds are here and people confidently come to stroke her, whereas when I'm out walking with her, some people would rather cross the road than be on the same side. However, as I said earlier, we are with a group of people who naturally love dogs and show no fear; dogs respect them for that.

We walk round the show many times, stopping now and again to watch the various classes. John and I even get to sit down and have a lovely cream tea and it's nice to sit and chill. We are feeling more relaxed and we're enjoying walking around looking at all the various stalls. We come across one that has doggie treat bags hidden just outside the stall and dogs are being invited to try to find one. It's no good asking Shy but we send Sheba in and after a good sniff around she finds one, picks it up and brings it over to us.

I hear the chap in charge say; "Well that's the best yet, we should take a photo". Sheba comes out sporting her trophy bag with the doggie treats inside. We are quite proud of her and both dogs will share the treats back home.

There are various activities for the dogs to try such as agility and a timed run. In the run, your dog has to stand at one end with you at the other, and when it's released it must run to you between two lines of fencing. John suggests I take Shy in to have a go. As she never leaves my side, he knows she will run straight to me. I'm not so sure but since there's no way she can get loose, I think she might enjoy a little blast off as she's been on the lead for quite a while. So leaving Shy with John, I walk to the other end, turn and call to her and sure enough she races towards me like a bullet shot from a gun. The only problem is the woman didn't start her stopwatch in time, so Shy hasn't been timed! She says we can do it again but I think it's enough; she's done really well and we don't want to push our luck.

As we leave, we're tired but very happy. Overall, I think our first show went really well. Shy got lots of attention from some very nice people, just what she needed to show her that not everyone is out to harm her. Before going home, we stop off at the field to let the dogs have a good run; Shy is always at her happiest in her own surroundings, she loves the field and it shows. It is after all, her place of safety. We spend the next day just quietly pottering around; I think the dogs like us, are in need of a rest and we have what I call a nothing day; just time to reflect on yesterday's events and chill out.

I'm still getting days when Shy is awkward about giving me her ball and about getting into the car. It's a sort of 'will she/won't she' game and I never know which mood is going to take her from day to day, it's all on her terms. I do know that if I let myself get annoyed, it will set her back and as we've come such a long way, I really don't want that to happen. I'll just have to resign myself to playing the waiting game and hope that whatever is upsetting her will eventually fade and she'll start to trust me again.

I decide to go back to playing with two balls, as I did when I first started teaching her to let go of the ball; she got the idea then so maybe she will again. This appears to work; for the moment anyway. I find too, that if I throw a piece of cheese (her absolute favourite treat) into the car first, it encourages her to jump in. It's hard to know what is going through her mind; she may be getting flashbacks to her earlier life, which scares her. Time is a great healer though and hopefully those frightening memories will eventually leave her.

Although there have been problems with getting in the car and releasing the ball, I can't fault Shy when it comes to her lessons. Her enthusiasm is amazing and I have to think of more and more things for her to learn. I've started teaching her the 'away' game, which is not coming easy to her as she still sticks as close as she can to my leg. I want her to gain the confidence to move away without thinking she has to be at my side all of the time, so teaching her this game might help. It's hard for her to understand what I want at first but by using her favourite 'cheese', placed by a small cone several feet away, she is starting to get the idea. When I shout 'Away' and point towards the cone, she runs towards it to retrieve her precious cheesy bits and I can see she's beginning to enjoy the game.

John starts to take Sheba to the field so I can concentrate on Shy's lessons; it's a lot easier when there's just one dog to deal with and both dogs enjoy getting individual attention from time to time. This morning though, we take both dogs for a nice walk through Trench Woods again and they have a lovely time. It's the one place where Shy does leave me, following Sheba and tracking all the new, different and exciting scents. I know they love their walks in the field but I'm sure they appreciate a change now and again.

Shy is now a lot more comfortable around John and now goes quite willingly into the garden with him. This morning, feeling in a confident mood, he decides to take the dogs to the field on his own. If this works, it'll take some of the load off me; there are times when I need a break. I help him load the dogs in the car, and stand watching as they drive away; both dogs' noses pressed up against the back window, watching me as they go. However, they're not gone long. Shy bolted for the gate when John let the dogs out and he was afraid she'd get out onto the road and run for home, so he put them straight back in the car and drove home. Oh well, it looks like it's not time for me to put my feet up just yet. We both take the dogs to the field with us in the afternoon and its obvious Shy is in a very happy mood. (Well happier than John's anyway!)

Trouble with the car this morning, I don't think it's the battery as the engine is turning over but it just won't start. I am glad the field is in walking distance or it would be more of a problem; I'll just walk the dogs there instead. Shy walks very nicely now; she's much more confident and no longer jumps at everything that passes. I think her trip to the show has helped; for the first time it feels like she's actually enjoying her walk and that in turn rubs off on me and all three of us have a lovely walk.

The weather is turning very hot and I've been riding Oliver in the evenings when it gets cooler. This works well as the dogs have their run in the morning and I don't feel guilty about leaving them at home when I ride in the evening.

The car won't start again this morning but I'm not too bothered; after the lovely walk we had yesterday, I'm quite looking forward to doing it again. Unfortunately, things don't go to plan. As we start out, I see there is another dog and its owner walking slightly ahead of us. Sheba starts to pull and gets very vocal, which she does when she gets excited. I look behind and realise we are being followed by yet another dog having its walk. This is not a good situation to be in, Sheba spots the other dog and begins to get really silly and I'm starting to think we'll have to turn round and go home. Sheba is very strong and I'm finding it hard to control her. In the end, I decide to stop so that the dog behind us can get past. I put my dogs into the 'sit' and hold on as tightly as I can.

Things are easier after that; Sheba settles and our walk continues. Out of the two, Shy has been the best behaved. She was edgy but she wasn't putting me under the same pressure as Sheba, which is good, as I don't think I can control two unruly dogs. I don't know why Sheba is behaving so out of character this morning; maybe it's the hot weather making her tetchy. I know I can get very irritable in the heat, so I guess dogs can too. I'm pleased to reach the field so we can all chill out and very relieved when the walk home is uneventful and enjoyable.

The rest of May goes by without much to report; Shy is getting the hang of the away game, which shows when we have our walks across the field. I say to her, "Shy away" and she is starting to leave me and to realise she is not actually glued to my leg. It's still a bit hit and miss with the ball commands but mostly she gives it back more times than not and I'm not having so much trouble with her getting in the car either. She just has funny moments when only Shy knows why she's being awkward. I can live with that though, we both have a lot to learn, but she's still the most adorable little dog on the planet.

June

Summer is finally here and we're having some very hot days, so I'm careful how much running around the dogs do. Shy will chase after the ball until she drops if I let her but Sheba is beginning to struggle as she has a very thick coat and the heat makes her pant a lot. So at the moment we walk more than we run but even that can be hard work, especially for me as I'm never at my best in hot weather. We play ball more in the evenings when it's cooler and it also helps to tire the dogs before bedtime. Apart from the heat, June starts well; Shy is better at getting in the car, albeit still with a bribe but whatever it takes, it's better than trying to force her in; that's a battle I can't win.

We do have a hiccup in the middle of the week. Shy does a wee in the kitchen after her breakfast, which is naughty as she'd already been outside. Then she refuses to get in the car to go to the field, which is very unusual, as I've never had a problem with getting her in the car at home. I wait and wait but she will just not get in, so rather than losing my cool, I decide to leave her at home and just take Sheba with me, hoping that tomorrow she'll realise she could miss out on her walk again and jump in promptly.

No such luck; Shy again refuses to get in the car and again, I leave her at home. My mind is working overtime, how do I get her out of this latest hang-up? I know she loves going to the field and nothing bad has happened to her in the car since we've had her. I don't know what is going on in her little mind but the walks across the field aren't the same without her. Sheba misses her and I too miss the little cling-on who always has to be by my side. A part of us is missing and we don't like it. While we're walking, I'm thinking of how to solve the problem. Of course I can always walk the dogs to the field but there will be times when she really has to get in the car and I need to know she's not going to mess around. The only thing I come up with is taking a few steps backwards and repeating the game of letting the dogs jump in and out of the car of their own free will as we did originally. It worked then; it might work again.

When we get home, I ask John to park the car on the front lawn, we open the rear door as before and leave the dogs to their own devices and sure enough, they start to jump in and out of the car again. It's lovely to watch and at least we can see she isn't afraid of the car; maybe it's being shut in that frightens her, perhaps she feels trapped? We'll never know what she has suffered in her past and can only try to ease her into a better present as gently as we can.

Success! Shy jumps into the car this morning and there is a lovely happy atmosphere as we drive to the field – our little dog is back with us and we're complete again. We have a lovely walk with Shy doing her usual thing of chasing her ball and running back with what looks like a huge grin on her face. She's happy, Sheba is happy and I'm very happy.

Shy's confidence is now beginning to show through and she's much better now when Janet and Rebecca are around. She stands nearer to them but if they move too close to her she lets out a little bark, which always makes us laugh; she's trying to sound tough but we know she isn't!

The grandchildren don't frighten her so much either, she's not spending so much time in her basket when they're with us and even approaches them. Having had Shy for quite a while now, we know how much courage that takes from her; she is doing really well.

Getting Attached

When we're at home, Shy is getting into the car well, but she's still a bit awkward in the field, I have to throw the ball in first and most of the time she will jump in after it. Today however, when I throw it, she makes a grab for it almost before it leaves my hand, so when she lands in the car it's already in her mouth. In fact, instead of the ball, she's got the rope attached to it and doesn't realise that my finger is attached to the rope. It's very painful and I don't know what to do. As I've said, when Shy sets her mind no amount of coaxing will change it; all she knows is that she's got her precious ball even if it's dangling from the end of a rope and she's not going to give it up for anything. She has a very strong grip on the rope and my finger and I can't get her to open her mouth. The more I try to persuade her, the stronger it gets and it's really starting to hurt. There's no way I can go home with a dog dangling on the end my finger, I can't drive, and I won't even be able to walk home. The truth is I can't get her out of the car; she just will not get out.

In a way, it's quite funny. All the times I've had problems getting her into the car and now I can't get her out. I sit for a while, needing to give this some thought. And then it comes to me – somewhere in the back of my mind I've heard that if you let out a loud squeal, the dog will release whatever its holding – to do with puppies or something. I know she's had lots of puppies, so maybe it'll mean something to her. Anything is worth a try, I'm getting desperate, and my finger is starting to go numb. I get as close as I can to her ear and let out a loud squeal. Wow, it works! Shy immediately releases the rope with my finger attached. What a relief – I'm free.

My finger is throbbing but is still in one piece, which I'm thankful for and we set off for home. At least I can see the funny side. It's a ridiculous picture; a dog hanging off its owner's finger – who would believe it! With this going through my mind, I start laughing and the dogs look at me strangely; they don't get the joke.

The weather is still very hot, the kind of heat that drains all your energy. The dogs are feeling it too so I give them both a bath today and it really perks them up. It doesn't do much for me though; just leaves me more drained than ever.

Shy is still a bit hit and miss getting in the car; she's usually good at home but can still be awkward when we're in the field. It just seems to be how the mood takes her. She is female after all; that might explain a lot.

Mathew, who is a barber by trade, came to cut my hair today; he's very useful when John and I need a haircut! I sit in the kitchen while he cuts and I'm surprised at Shy's reaction; she jumps out of her basket, barking and barking at Mathew. I think she thinks he's hurting me; she's definitely getting braver.

Shy is putting on weight and is starting to look more like a Labrador. I need to watch that she doesn't put too much on though; I know Labradors have a tendency to get fat. She really loves her food and of course because of her background, I suspect I spoil her a bit but she does use up a lot of energy chasing her ball, so that should help.

Daniel pops round to see us and he brings a dog with him, a recent addition to Michelle's parent's family. He's a sweet little border collie-cross they have adopted from a dog re-homing centre. He's about twelve months old and is as mad as they come. I think Michelle's parents are finding him a bit of a handful and are trying to get Daniel and Michelle to take him on but their dog Lucky hasn't taken to him very well, I think he is just too lively. Daniel isn't keen on him anyway; he's just not Daniel's sort of dog. I think the idea might be to 'take him round to mum's, she won't be able to resist him' and the truth of the matter is, I would be tempted if we hadn't already got Shy but he'd be too much for her to cope with. Sheba is having great fun running around with him but I think even she would soon get tired of his endless zest for life, he needs loads of exercise. Maybe agility training would be his thing, something to channel his surplus energy. Shy is very nervous the whole time he's with us and is very relieved when he goes home.

The Kick

Sometimes I ride out with our neighbour and her daughter. They're bringing on a young horse and it's always useful to ride with a more experienced horse to show the youngster the ropes. We've ridden out several times and he's coming on well so today we've arranged to go out again – Michelle riding her horse Jazz; daughter Ellie on Harry the youngster, and me on Oliver. The ride is going well but I must have taken my eye off the ball for a moment and Oliver spun round on the spot, nearly dumping me onto the ground. He had spotted what I should have noticed – Harry taking a well-aimed kick at him. Luckily, due to Oliver's quick thinking, the kick misses him and catches my foot instead. In a way, I'm pleased it was me he kicked and not Oliver because where it would have landed might have been very painful for him.

We continue our ride with no further incidents. My foot is hurting but not too badly. It's only when we get home and I take my boot off that the real pain hits. I've had many kicks and falls in the years I've owned horses; it comes with the territory but this really hurts – the pain is awful and I can hardly walk. He must have hit the bone and there's not much flesh on a foot so it can be extremely painful. I can't do much walking at all in the next few days.

John takes on the chore of checking the horses while I try and rest my foot but Sheba decides to stay at home with me and won't go with him. She does this now and again and I always say she is in one of her clingy moods but maybe this time she's staying to look after me, she knows I'm hurting; Shy of course stays as well.

My foot starts to feel a bit better, so I can go back to checking the horses and do short walks around the field. The dogs are very happy to get their old routine back even though they aren't getting much of a walk.

We have another visit from Daniel who comes on his own this time. He makes a point of going up to Shy and talking to her whenever he visits and this time when he strokes her, she lets him. This is a big step forward for her; she's beginning to trust him, just a little.

I'm walking more now and my foot is on the mend. I can't say its right but it does feel a lot better. As I'm not limping anymore and the dogs have missed out lately, we take them to the Countryside Centre. No problems getting them in or out of the car this time; I think they are just too excited to be going out for Shy to mess around; she's well and truly up for having some fun. Even though my foot is aching, we have a lovely walk and meet quite a few people with dogs. Shy is noticeably more relaxed on this visit to the centre; I think her trust in us is really starting to grow.

The Dog's Trust have their show today and we'd love to take the dogs but it's a long way to travel and could be too much for Shy to cope with. We're not sure how she would react to going back to the centre anyway. She might think we're taking her back and I don't think she'd like that; all her worries might come flooding back. We can't take that chance and I think we've made the right decision.

In the summer, we section the field to grow some of the grass for hay and leave the horses to graze down the rest. The hay is their food for the winter when the grazing is poor. Now however, the grass is so tall, it's getting awkward for the dogs and I to walk through; sometimes Shy disappears completely from sight. Her legs aren't as long as Sheba's and all I can see is the tip of her tail. We spend a lot of time searching for lost balls and I'm sure they do it deliberately because it always seems to happen when our walk is almost over and they know we're heading for the car; hunting for lost balls helps to prolong the walk! It's interesting watching the dogs' individual techniques for tracking their balls; Sheba runs up and down nose to the ground until she finds the scent, whereas Shy runs round and round in ever decreasing circles until she finds her ball. She's really learning how to use her nose now, in the early days she hadn't got a clue but I think by watching Sheba she's learnt a lot.

The stream is running very low; we've had no rain for quite a while now and the dogs can't get the swim they so badly need to cool off in the heat. To make up for it, I spray them with the hosepipe when we get home; they don't enjoy it half as much as splashing around in the stream but it does help to cool them off. Perhaps we should get them a paddling pool.

June has ended and another month has gone by of learning and enjoying the company of our little companion. As always, I'm looking forward to the next month to see how Shy moves on with her life.

July

July starts well; Shy gives me her ball now with no fuss at all, so maybe she has passed through that awkward phase at last. Sheba and Shy love their playtimes, chasing the balls, there's never any aggression, they just enjoy playing with each other and I never tire of watching them having fun. Shy has a true friend at last; she's so lucky to have such a very special companion as Sheba.

The grass still hasn't been cut for hay, so we can only play ball in the schooling area where it's nice and short. My foot still aches; some days worse than others but now, my hip is starting to hurt as well. I've had operations on both my hips and I get worried if I have pain in case it means something is wrong. I just hope it's due to walking awkwardly because of my foot and not anything more serious. Not being able to walk the whole field at the moment is actually better for me because I'm not putting so much pressure on the injured foot. The dogs don't seem too bothered as long as they are able to play; I think even they might find it hard covering the whole field while the weather is so very hot.

Shy's getting in the car much better which is a relief; we're moving forward again and her confidence is coming on in leaps and bounds. She even barked at Janet and didn't back away this time but stood her ground; good to see in a dog as badly traumatised as Shy. It isn't the sort of thing I would encourage in a normal well-adjusted dog but with Shy it is different, she's beginning to come out of her very dark shell.

I still have real problems with my foot and John wants me to go to the doctor in case I've cracked a bone or something. I don't think I have, but it is going on a bit, so I get an appointment for tomorrow. The doctor doesn't think I've broken anything but says he thinks the foot is badly bruised and it will just take time for it to get better. Oh well, it's put John's mind at rest anyway.

Shy is getting on better with Buffy and I'm so pleased with how she's doing in general, that we decide to take her to a small dog show this coming Sunday.

The heat wave continues and today's forecast is for the hottest day of the year so far and I feel sorry for the horses as they'll be very uncomfortable if it's right. I think the only creatures that really enjoy this kind of weather are flies, which torment the poor horses and I've never found a fly spray yet that truly works. The only real relief they get is when they take refuge in their shelters. I feel sorry for horses that don't have shelters or hedges to give them shade, it must be awful for them; I find horses tend to use their shelters more in summer than in winter, seeming to cope better with cold than too much heat.

My foot is finally starting to improve; which helps a lot when playing with the dogs and seeing to the horses.

After the hottest day of the year, the next day brings rain; it just pours down and it's such a relief. The dogs and I revel in getting soaked to the skin and loving every minute. I hope it stops tomorrow though as it's the day of the dog show.

We wake up this morning happy to see the weather is fine and after all yesterday's rain everything feels fresh and clean. When we've walked the dogs, we get ourselves ready and head for the show. The journey goes well with no messes from Shy and we hope she'll remember going the first time and perhaps enjoy herself a bit more today.

The show is busy with dogs and people everywhere and I know this is difficult for Shy but undeterred, I pop her lead and vest on and confidently stride towards the show ground, hoping she'll catch my mood and shed her anxieties. John and Sheba lead the way again and Shy does better; she's not quite as jumpy as the first time. She still doesn't like it when people are on both sides of us but where there's a bit of space, she starts to relax a bit and take in her surroundings.

John and I do the same as we did before; walking round the show ring several times, stopping now and then to look at some of the classes and checking out the various stalls. After a while, we sit down by the edge of a large pool at a short distance from the main arena, which gives us a chance to watch everything going on and means Shy can sit and relax without the stress of the crowds. She seems to appreciate the break and is more relaxed when we walk round again. We don't stay too long at the show, just enough for Shy to get used to mixing with other dogs and of course, their humans.

We're really pleased with how the dogs behave themselves. John comments that Shy is so much better than at the last show, and it's been well worth bringing her. The journey back is uneventful and before going home, we take the dogs to the field again to let off steam. Although it might appear to be a bit of a bother to take Shy to shows, it's an important part of her rehabilitation process and as long as it doesn't cause her unnecessary stress I think it will help to introduce her to the outside world, where she can see the happier side of life for herself.

She does seem more settled today, so I think taking her to the show has been good for her. The weather is very hot again so I'm still not letting the dogs do much running around. We're all still a bit tired from yesterday anyway, so we have an easy, quiet day.

It's my birthday – and guess what – the grass is being cut today; I watch my two beautiful dogs running about and playing about like a couple of kids enjoying the great outdoors and I think this is the best birthday present I could wish for. The field looks huge now and I can give the dogs a proper run. They're so excited that even the heat doesn't seem to bother them; It's as if a completely new world has opened up for them and I watch as they run here and there, quartering the whole field until they have checked out every scent. They even manage to paddle, despite there being only a trickle of water in the stream. Life is good again and I have two very contented dogs by the time we head for home. They spend the rest of the day lying in their baskets; I think the heat has finally caught up with them.

Rebecca and her husband have just bought a puppy, a Golden Retriever, about eleven weeks old. Rebecca's going to pop in and show it to us while she's visiting her parents; we only live a couple of doors away from their house. Like all puppies, he is gorgeous; quite big for his age and I think he will be a big boy when he's fully grown. We bring Sheba and Shy out of the house to meet him. I think Shy will enjoy seeing him; he's a puppy and she knows all about them! Sheba gets on really well with him, happily following the excited little fellow around but when he goes over to meet Shy, she snaps at him, making him squeal. Maybe puppies aren't her thing after all; I can understand if she wants to leave that part of her life well and truly behind.

Shy is nervous of Buffy today and I think perhaps meeting Oscar the puppy yesterday has set her back a bit but she puts it all behind her, running after her ball in her newly reclaimed field. She really comes to life when she's free, throwing off the chains that bound her so cruelly for all those years. As I watch her I can feel her spirit rising, energy exploding out of her body; this little dog is coming back to life before my very eyes.

The hay has been gathered and made into fifty-four large round bales; the horses will have plenty to eat this winter that's for sure. I walk the dogs to the highest point where we can see the whole of the field and sit down on the grass; the dogs come and lie by my side and we just sit, looking across it. It's a perfect moment; just the three of us lost in our own little world, quite content to just enjoy the peace and quiet of our field this morning. It's like looking at an old oil painting with the sun shining gently down on the hay bales scattered across the field; birds are singing, bees are buzzing and we even spot a deer looking around, perhaps wondering where all his camouflage has gone; there's nowhere for him to hide now the grass is cut. I don't want Sheba to chase him so I hold on to her collar until he's out of sight but she seems quite happy to just stay with me, soaking up the atmosphere. Sitting there, I start thinking how nice it would be to paint a picture of this; it would be lovely to save the memory of the moment. I'll ask John to come back with me to take some photos before the bales are collected. So we have two walks this morning, and John took some great photos of the dogs and me playing hide and seek in between the bales. The hay is collected later that afternoon so I am very glad the photos were taken; I'm sure there will be some good ones I can use when I'm in the right mood for painting.

With the bales gone, the field looks very large and bare. There's a bench at the very end and now that the grass is nice and short, I can walk to it easily. I call it my healing bench and it's where I rest and spend quiet moments, allowing me to free my mind and experience the mystical sensation I always feel when I am in this place. For this short period in time, I feel completely at one with nature. The dogs lie by my feet enjoying their own rest before we continue on our walk.

It's the last day in July and poor Sheba has an upset stomach; she has quite a sensitive stomach, unlike Shy, who is always 'fit as a butcher's dog', as the saying goes. If she hadn't been such a tough little cookie, I don't think she would have survived but she did, and I'm very thankful for it. Watching this little dog evolving before my eyes is something I shall always be grateful for; she's shown me the true meaning of guts, a real little fighter with a heart of gold.

August

We have the grandchildren twice in the first week of August. Ellie is really starting to come out of her shell now and they both enjoy coming to see us and of course, the dogs. I keep finding them stroking and talking to Shy as she lies in her basket but she knows now that they won't hurt her and I think secretly she enjoys the attention.

Shy's booster injections are due and I've made an appointment for Wednesday. I must admit I am not looking forward to it; we can't even take Sheba in with us as she hates it at the vets and gets very vocal waiting her turn in the waiting room, which won't help Shy at all, so I know I'll have to take her in on her own. I explain Shy's problem to them and arrange to have the first appointment, hoping we'll have the waiting room to ourselves. We arrive with time to spare so we give the dogs a little walk before John takes Sheba back to the car and I head for the surgery. At the door Shy is very reluctant to follow me in, continually looking around for Sheba; when she realises Sheba isn't coming with us, she reluctantly follows me and we go through a second door into the waiting room.

As we enter the waiting room, my heart sinks; the room is full of people, mostly men. It appears they're having a meeting before the surgery opens. This is too much for Shy, who panics, crouches down, and wees on the floor. The girl behind the desk notices and quickly ushers us into a very small room and leaves us there on our own.

I've brought a bag of cheesy treats with me, which I know Shy loves and I sit stroking and talking to her, wondering if she will take one. Previously she hasn't been able to eat when she's under stress like this and at first she is reluctant but we spend about ten minutes in the room and it gives her enough time to relax a bit enabling her to enjoy her favourite treats.

By the time the vet calls us in, the time we've had on our own has done us both good and we've calmed down a bit. Shy follows me in and stands quite calmly on the scales when I ask her to. The vet says she's a bit overweight, which actually makes me smile, remembering the skinny little waif of eleven months earlier. She's checked all over and given a clean bill of health; out comes the needle and in the wink of an eye, it's all over. There are no problems getting her back in the car; I think we'd have had trouble trying to keep her out; she's more than happy to be going home. We stop on the way back and take the dogs for a lovely walk around the Countryside Centre and I don't know who appreciates it more, me or Shy, we both need to chill out.

We have a lovely quiet day today after our ordeal; there are no ill effects from Shy's injection and overall I think everything went well.

Buffy's Holiday

Caroline is going on holiday for a week so we're going to look after Buffy. I'm not sure how Shy will react to having her around all day and night. It might be too much for her to cope with but they've been getting on much better lately, so hopefully, I'm worrying for nothing. John checks the horses for me, taking Sheba with him, while I stay and play ball with Shy until it's time for Buffy to arrive. When John comes back, he says that Sheba ran at some people who were crossing the field; he hadn't seen them quickly enough. She didn't do them any harm, just frightened them a bit. It's a shame, as she hasn't done anything like that for a long time. I do notice though, that she is not as relaxed with John and if she's going to play up, it's usually when she's with him. Maybe he's not quite so confident with her and she picks up on it.

Buffy will sleep in the back porch; we don't think it is a good idea to put them all in the kitchen, in case something upsets them in the night and I know Shy won't sleep very well if Buffy's in the same room with her. Buffy is very good through the night, no noise and no messes in the morning so the day starts well. Apart from the weather that is, it's pouring down, too bad to take the dogs to the field, so good old John checks the horses again for me. It brightens up in the afternoon and I walk Shy to the field while John takes the other two in the car; we didn't think it would be wise to put all three in the car together and it's doubtful if we could get Shy in the car with Buffy there anyway. This is the first time I've walked Shy to the field without Sheba and I'm not sure what to expect but she's brilliant. Afterwards, John walks Buffy home and the others come back with me in the car. It couldn't have gone better, Shy doesn't seem too worried about having Buffy around and they're getting on well with each other. They all seemed to enjoy the walk and things are going well so far.

Caroline has had Buffy for quite a while now but she's never been able to teach her to sit or lie down. She thinks that Buffy's long gangly legs make it difficult for her, but as she's leaving, she says; "Can you teach Buffy to sit mum?"

As if I haven't enough to do already! However, I've got my orders and when tea time comes I ask Buffy to sit. She's quite stubborn and just gives me a very defiant look. I ask her again, this time holding the dish above her head. As she looks up, I say "sit" again and gently push on her bottom and she sort of does a half sit. I give her loads of praise and then let her have her tea. I am very pleased with that; she met me half way and tomorrow I might even get a full sit.

The weather is better this morning, so Shy and I walk to the field again, while John drives down with the other two. Shy is very good, especially as most of the way, there's another dog being taken for a walk in front of us but she doesn't pull me at all; she is such a good dog.

Buffy's really getting the hang of sitting and I am amazed how quickly she is learning – I even start teaching her to lie down. This dog is bright – brighter than Caroline I suspect.

Today Sheba and Shy have their first punch-up. It just came out of the blue and I don't know what started it; maybe it's because Buffy is staying with us and their routine has been altered. Luckily, it doesn't last long and I hope it's a one-off. They've been so well with each other up to now, it would be such a shame if things are about to change. I hope that a good run in the field will help them forget their differences.

For a change this morning, John walks Buffy to the field while Sheba and Shy come with me in the car. The walk goes well, with no signs of any friction; in fact, they all seem to be enjoying each other's company and I hope that whatever upset them yesterday is now forgotten. I walk Shy home and she does very well but still gets frightened when we meet anyone.

We plan to do the same today with me walking Shy home again but she has a different plan and surprises us both by jumping in the car with the other two; she obviously doesn't want to walk home today. The three dogs travel well in the car together with no signs of any friction between them. OK, if I manage to get the dogs in the car tomorrow, I'll take them all to the field.

Brilliant! All three dogs jump in the car this morning. It does cross my mind that there might be problems getting Shy back in at home-time if she has one of her awkward moments but I needn't have worried because she's the first to get in.

Buffy doesn't fetch balls but she does love chasing furry animals like rabbits and squirrels. She never manages to catch one but I think if I throw something soft for her, maybe she'd be more inclined to run after it. So armed with a soft Frisbee toy and a ball for Sheba, I take the two dogs into the back garden and start playing fetch with Sheba. Buffy starts to get excited, so when Sheba comes back with her ball I hold her collar and throw the soft Frisbee, saying, "Fetch" to Buffy who races after it and picks it up. She then runs round and round the garden, not coming back to me, which I didn't expect but she is having a really good time on her own. I think if Caroline wants to teach her to play ball then this is the way to go.

Today is our last day with Buffy. Janet's son David and his girlfriend come to the field to see Swampy the horse. They haven't met Shy or Buffy before and are much taken with Buffy – Shy however, gives them a wide birth.

When Caroline comes to pick Buffy up after her holiday, I hand her some cheesy bits and say; "Ask your dog to sit." She looks at me with surprise, I don't think she really believes me but she does as I say and sure enough, Buffy sits. I don't think Caroline can believe her eyes. "She can lie down as well!" I add so she asks her for a down and Buffy obliges. "And she can shake a paw." I say. This is all too much for Caroline to take in; she's over the moon. Apparently, the next day, when she's out walking Buffy, she stops to talk to various people and tells them about Buffy's newly acquired skills and gets her to perform. I hope Buffy enjoyed all the attention.

It seems very quiet in the field this morning without Buffy; I've got quite used to having three dogs with me and I keep thinking one has gone missing. The dogs seem to have a good time though, and Shy gets in the car with no fuss. Shy is much more relaxed now when she meets Buffy in the garden; I think it's done them both good to spend the week together.

Celebration Time

It's our 50th wedding anniversary today – quite some achievement! I feel I've known John all my life and I wouldn't have it any other way, I've been so lucky. He has always been there for me, encouraging and supporting me in whatever I've chosen to do. He is my soul mate and I feel really blessed.

Because I'm in a particularly good mood this morning, I give the dogs a treat and take them for a run through Trench Woods before going to the field. They're well up for this and I think they really enjoy the change, there are so many different scents to follow and they disappear into their own world, just doing what comes naturally to them.

We decide to celebrate our anniversary on Saturday with a BBQ in the field. All the children and grandchildren will be with us and everyone will be able to let off steam, and of course, all the dogs will come too.

Saturday arrives. The forecast is not too bad but the weather doesn't look very promising. The forecasters got it wrong again and John and I dodge the showers as we try to set everything up in the field; it's not even very warm either. We aren't sure how Shy will cope with the festivities but we are definitely taking her and if she finds it too much, we'll pop her back home. At least it's dry when everybody arrives and nobody but John and me seems to be bothering about the weather.

We all have a great time, even though it takes John ages to light the BBQ and the bonfire never really gets going. The grandchildren run around nonstop, playing lots of games and its lovely having all our family together; healthy, happy and having fun. We are so lucky.

Shy surprises us most of all when she joins in a game of football, I think she sees Sheba having fun and doesn't want to miss out, so a good time is had by all. It's dark by the time we leave the field; except for the bonfire, which has just burst into life. Oh well, not everything goes to plan; we are all tired but very, very happy.

The dogs are tired today after our very busy day and late night and Shy seems in a calm mood, I think yesterday's events did her good. Because we're having an easy day, I take the opportunity for a ride out on Oliver which I enjoy and I think he does too.

The weather is wet for the rest of the week but the dogs never seem to mind getting wet. Shy still loves her jumping so I put some small ones up in the garden again; she flies over them and so does Sheba, determined she is never going to get left behind.

Another Show Under Her Collar

There's a dog show at the Blue Cross rescue centre on Saturday, and weather permitting, we're going to take the dogs. It's a bit further to travel than the other two but I don't see that as a problem anymore.

Saturday arrives and the weather is overcast but dry, so we get the dogs ready and set off for the show. All seems to be going well until Shy decides to have a wee and makes a mess in the car; she's not as ready as I had thought. When it's safe enough to stop the car, I have the chore of squeezing in the back and cleaning up as best as I can. It's not for the faint hearted I can tell you but with the car smelling a bit fresher, we carry on to the show.

It's quite a relief when we get there and there's no hesitation from any of us in jumping out of the car and gulping in the fresh air. I put Shy's vest on and leaving the car with all the windows slightly open, we head for the show.

Shy gets a lot of attention while we're waiting in the long queue for the showground and everybody seems very interested in her story. They all feel very sorry for her and one man even manages to stroke her. This makes his day and every time we bump into him around the ground, he makes a point of stopping and talking to her. I'm not sure if Shy really enjoys the attention but it is the sort of thing she needs and seeing Sheba receiving attention and fuss with no objection, it must be a good example for her.

Caroline is also at the show, selling her plants from a stall and it's nice to go and have a chat now and again, it breaks the day up. Again, we're very pleased with the dogs, Shy especially is coping really well, much braver now than at the other shows we've taken her to; she still has a long way to go but she is definitely going in the right direction. The return journey goes well with no more accidents in the car which does smell a bit fresher, but it'll still need a good clean out when we get home.

The dogs get a well-earned rest today; John and I have arranged to visit his brother and wife, who live in Sutton Coldfield. It's quite a journey and we know we'll be leaving the dogs for several hours. I am a bit worried about Shy, she's never been left for so long before but there has to be a first time and I know Sheba won't worry. She knows we'll be coming back and hopefully she'll communicate that to Shy.

Shy does look very relieved when we get home and Sheba does her usual excited barking act. I get loads of hugs from Shy; they are both very glad to see us.

Shy is a bit clingy today, maybe because she missed us yesterday. How could I ever think of leaving this dog? It would break her brave little heart – she'll just have to spend enough time with us for her to trust that we are not going anywhere.

Now that her confidence is growing, I notice that Shy is starting to pull when she's on the lead; I'll do more heel-work practice with her; I know she can walk to heel beautifully and I don't want her to lose it.

Caroline's having problems getting Buffy into her car to go home; she enjoyed her holiday with us so much that she wants to stay here. She will only get into the car when I tell her to. I'm sure it will dawn on her soon that the holiday is over and she really has got to go home.

Shy has to go to the vet for a second injection; for some reason she has two this year but only one a year after that. I'm not looking forward to it but hope she'll remember her last visit when nothing awful happened and be more relaxed. I arrange for an early appointment again and this time, the waiting room is empty – we're the only ones here. Shy behaves very well with no accidents this time. She's always had two quite big lumps on her side, so I ask the vet to look at them and tell me what she thinks. She asks if they've been getting any bigger but they haven't, so she just says to keep an eye on them; if they do start to grow, we should take her back straight away, and she will look again.

I always thought the Dogs Trust would have told us when we adopted her if they'd thought it was something to worry about, so I'm relieved for now and will push it to the back of my mind and just accept it as part of Shy, like the scar by her eye. The marks are there as a reminder of her past and will always be with her. I'm very happy with how the visit goes, much better than last time. To finish on a good note, we all have a lovely walk at the Countryside Centre.

The blacksmith is due this week and I take the dogs with me when he comes. Sheba of course has met him before but it will be a first for Shy, who barks at him; she couldn't have done that a few months ago. Otherwise, they are both very good.

August is almost at an end and it feels we've had quite a busy month, what with vet visits, Buffy's holiday with us and the dog show; not to mention the anniversary party! Shy has been doing really well but she still has some off days and I guess these will continue for some time yet. The good days are becoming much more frequent though and hopefully it won't be too long before the bad memories are just that; a thing of the past.

Our First Year Comes to an End

September

It is almost twelve months since we anxiously brought our shy girl home, the brave little dog who stole our hearts.

Back then, we worried so much if we'd be capable of giving her the life she needed so badly. That has long since passed and this little dog has been a joy to live with. And it's been a two way thing, Shy herself has taught me so much; making me dig deeply inside to come up with the right way to help her overcome her fears and to exercise patience I didn't know I had. This and the overall feel-good factor are just a few of the ways Shy has helped me. She's quite a different animal now from when we first brought her home, yes, she's still very nervous of people but who can blame her for that? How she ever accepted me as her friend never fails to amaze me and now the closeness to John is starting to form.

It's hard to believe how much this dog has learnt in just twelve months. She came to us with absolutely nothing; her life until then was just bare existence and nothing else. Shy is an extremely intelligent animal and to suppress that must have been awful. Perhaps it was because of her spark that she did survive; taking herself off into her own little world and hiding there just as if she had closed down. Hoarding her spirit was the only way to cope with the cruelty she was suffering; the only way she stayed alive.

I know I have helped with Shy's rebirth but a lot of the credit should go to our other beautiful dog Sheba. Without her kindness, understanding and patience, Shy would not be the dog she is today. She's learnt so much from watching Sheba;

things only a dog could show her, and we work well as a team. Sheba teaches her the doggie side of life, and I try and show her the better side of human nature. Together we have watched our little protégé unfold and she has turned into a dog anyone would be proud to own. In a different life, I think Shy should have excelled at anything she was asked to do, whether it is agility, obedience, or even helping a disabled person. Given the right training, I know she would give her heart and soul; I count myself a very lucky person to have the privilege of her in my life.

We first saw Shy on Friday 13th 2013, she is also the 13th dog John and I have owned. Thirteen must be a lucky number for us and for Shy as well.

If nothing else comes from this book, I hope it will give some people the courage to re-home a dog with special needs. It's been perfect for John and me because we are pensioners, with time and a lot of experience to draw on. The many dogs we've had during our lives have all helped us in rehabilitating Shy. If not for them, we wouldn't have had the knowledge or expertise to help this dog. I trust there are many kind-hearted people out there who, like us, would benefit greatly from the rewards a needy pet can give.

I hope we have many more years with Shy and I look forward to them all even though I know she'll always keep me on my toes. I'm sure there will be many more problems for me to solve and a lot more energy to find, keeping up with her never-ending lust for life.

I feel a pet is given to you for a reason and Shy has helped me to find the real me, to feel more comfortable with my inner self, not to take life too seriously and to live for the moment, just like she has done. Shy has taught me a lot and the two of us have helped each other in so many ways. I'd love to believe that if Shy could talk she'd turn her little head, look me in the eye and say, "It's good to be SHY".

EPILOGUE

Two Years Later

S hy has been with us for three years now and it would be good to say that she's now a very well-adjusted dog whose fear of people is long forgotten but that's not the case. She will never completely forget the cruelty she received all those years ago. But, with all that, she is the sweetest little dog that ever lived. Her devotion to me is incredible, something that few people ever experience in their lives. I've been lucky enough to receive this not just from one dog but two; Shy and Sheba my beautiful Shepherd, between them give me such undying loyalty and love that it never ceases to amaze me. These two dogs have brought unimaginable happiness into my life, I look forward to every new day, knowing the time we spend together will never fail to cheer me up and make me laugh; life will never be dull with these two around to keep me on my toes.

Shy is nine and Sheba is a grand old lady of eleven now and between us we're all starting to slow down a little. Shy still loves her ball games, but she stops more often now to catch her breath. Sheba is more content to sit and watch Shy do the running around, but every now and then, she still has to prove to Shy she can get to the ball first; and for her age she has still got incredible speed. I am very lucky that both my dogs are very healthy and I look forward to many more years with them. There are no more problems getting Shy in the car now, that's all a thing of the past, Buffy often comes with us on our walks and the dogs enjoy being together.

Apart from her fear of people, Shy has few problems now, she loves life and it shows; she is very close to John and he loves her. I'd like to think that one day his very own dog will come along and he too can experience the joy I've had from that 'special' bond.

We're down to three horses now since we lost Little Lady; we are left with just Rosa, Oliver and Frisbee. Poor Frisbee misses his little soul mate, as they were inseparable but he and I are closer than we've ever been; Rosa is still a martyr to her arthritis but stiffness apart, she looks well for her age and still manages to put Oliver in his place when needed. Oliver, I call my Peter Pan; he's twenty four (going on five) but never acts his age and I hope he never does. He's a joy to watch as he struts his stuff, showing off and dancing around the field. I still love riding him and I hope we can carry on for a good while yet.

The past three years have been very special for John and me; neither of us could have known how much pleasure we would get from taking in this very traumatised little dog. To be able to watch her develop into a fun loving, happy and devoted friend has been more than enough reward. Would we do it again? YES, WE WOULD.

www.ingramcontent.com/pod-product-compliance
Lightning Source LLC
Chambersburg PA
CBHW032032040426
42449CB00007B/870